The Double-Decker Bus

Early Addition and Subtraction

Maarten Dolk

Nina Liu

Catherine Twomey Fosnot

firsthand
An imprint of Heinemann
A division of Reed Elsevier, Inc.
361 Hanover Street
Portsmouth, NH 03801–3912
firsthand.heinemann.com

Offices and agents throughout the world

ISBN 13: 978-0-325-01008-3
ISBN 10: 0-325-01008-0

Harcourt School Publishers
6277 Sea Harbor Drive
Orlando, FL 32887–6777
www.harcourtschool.com

ISBN 13: 978-0-15-360560-4
ISBN 10: 0-15-360560-X

© 2007 Catherine Twomey Fosnot

The development of a portion of the material described within was supported in part by the National Science Foundation under Grant No. 9911841. Any opinions, findings, and conclusions or recommendations expressed in these materials are those of the authors and do not necessarily reflect the views of the National Science Foundation.

Library of Congress Cataloging-in-Publication Data
CIP data is on file with the Library of Congress

Printed in the United States of America on acid-free paper

2013   FP   1 2 3 4

Acknowledgements

Literacy Consultant

Nadjwa E.L. Norton
Childhood Education, City College of New York

Photography

Herbert Seignoret
Mathematics in the City, City College of New York

Illustrator

Stacy Schuett

Schools featured in photographs:

The Muscota New School/PS 314 (an empowerment school in Region 10), New York, NY
Independence School/PS 234 (Region 9), New York, NY
Fort River Elementary School, Amherst, MA

Contents

Unit Overview

This unit begins with the story of a double-decker bus—a bus that has two decks with ten seats on each. Five seats on each deck are red and five seats are white. The bus goes by quickly and the little girl in the story, sitting at her bedroom window and watching, works out ways to use the colors of the seats to calculate quickly how many people are on the bus. Her father drives a double-decker bus and she helps him figure out a way to know how many empty seats there are on the top deck even though he can't see them.

The unit introduces the arithmetic rack as a powerful model and tool to act out the story. The arithmetic rack is a calculating frame consisting of two rows

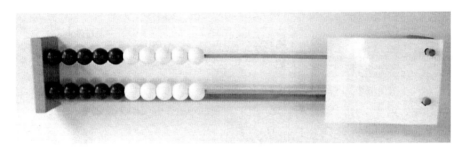

The Landscape of Learning

BIG IDEAS

- ☀ Cardinality
- ☀ Hierarchical inclusion
- ☀ Unitizing
- ☀ The relationship between addition and subtraction

- ☀ One-to-one correspondence
- ☀ Compensation and equivalence
- ☀ Commutativity and associativity

STRATEGIES

- ☀ Using synchrony and one-to-one tagging
- ☀ Counting on and counting backward
- ☀ Using trial and adjustment vs. systematic exploration
- ☀ Using compensation

- ☀ Counting three times
- ☀ Using the five- and ten-structures
- ☀ Using doubles and near doubles
- ☀ Making tens

MODEL

- ☀ Arithmetic rack

of ten beads—two sets of five (one red and one white) in each row. (Instructions for creating or buying your own arithmetic racks are included on page 75.)

Cognitive psychologists have shown that even toddlers can recognize small amounts, such as two or three, as a unit and that this ability (known as "subitizing") is probably innate (Dehaene 1999). Children can even do addition and subtraction with amounts of this size because they use this innate perceptual ability to see that three is one more than two. Using the arithmetic rack allows kindergarteners and first graders to build on their natural ability and see five as a unit. When five can be subitized as a whole, it can be used to support understanding of 6 as 5 + 1, 8 as 5 + 3, or 4 as 5 − 1. The arithmetic rack also supports the strategies of doubles and near doubles, 6 + 7 = 6 + 6 + 1, and making tens, 9 + 6 = 10 + 5.

In this unit, children move the beads on the arithmetic rack to represent passengers going from one deck on the bus to the other, and sitting in various combinations in the red and white seats. This context supports the development of the understanding that numbers can be named in many ways, for example 10 as 6 + 4, 7 + 3, or 5 + 5. The unit also includes minilessons with quick images, and strings of related addition and subtraction problems solved with the arithmetic rack to help automatize the basic facts.

Several games—Passenger Pairs, Rack Pairs, and Passenger Combos—are also included in this unit. They can be played throughout the year as a way for children to extend composing and decomposing strategies as they establish equivalence—for example, representing 7 as 5 + 2, 3 + 4, or 1 + 6 (Treffers 1991).

The Mathematical Landscape

The mathematical focus of this unit is early number sense. One of the manipulatives introduced is the arithmetic rack. The arithmetic rack (the Dutch term is *rekenrek*) was developed by Adri Treffers, a researcher at the Freudenthal Institute in the Netherlands. Based on much developmental research, the arithmetic rack was designed to align with children's early number sense strategies, enabling them to move from counting one by one to decomposing and composing number with subunits (Treffers 1991). The arithmetic rack encourages the automatizing of the basic facts by focusing on relationships and the use of strategies such as doubles and near doubles (8 + 7 = 7 + 7 + 1) and making tens (9 + 7 = 10 + 6). In contrast, the use of counters alone may keep children at the stage of counting by ones.

BIG IDEAS

This unit is designed to encourage the development of some of the big ideas underlying early number sense, including:

❖ *cardinality*

❖ *one-to-one correspondence*

❖ *hierarchical inclusion*

❖ *compensation and equivalence*

❖ *unitizing*

❖ *commutativity and associativity*

❖ *the relationship between addition and subtraction*

❖ Cardinality

Young children often count by rote without understanding the purpose of counting. They may not have constructed the big idea of cardinality—that the number they end on is the number of objects in the set. Thus, when children finish counting, it is important to ask, "So how many do you have?" Don't assume that because they seem to count well they understand that 8 means eight objects. They may think the eighth object is 8.

❖ One-to-one correspondence

One-to-one correspondence requires that children understand that if there are two groups and if each object in one group is paired with an object in the other group, then the groups each contain the same number of objects.

❖ Hierarchical inclusion

Even when children do understand cardinality and one-to-one correspondence, they still may not realize that the numbers grow by one, and exactly one, each time. Researchers call this idea hierarchical inclusion

(Kamii 1985). They mean that amounts nest inside each other: six includes five, plus one; five includes four, plus one, etc. This concept underlies the making ten strategy and the use of doubles to solve near-doubles problems. For example, to use 10 + 6 to solve 9 + 7, children need to understand that there is 1 more in the 7 than in the 6, and that the 1, when given to the 9, results in 10.

❖ Compensation and equivalence

Children may initially have a difficult time comprehending that 5 + 3 is equivalent to 4 + 4. The big ideas here are compensation and equivalence—that if you lose one (from the five, for example) but gain it (onto the three), the total stays the same. These big ideas, once constructed, allow children to realize that a problem like 6 + 8 can be solved with a double, 7 + 7.

❖ Unitizing

Unitizing requires that children use number to count not only objects but also groups—and to count them both simultaneously. For young learners, unitizing is a shift in perspective. Children have just learned to count ten objects, one by one. Unitizing these ten objects as *one* thing—one group—challenges their original idea of number. How can something be ten and one at the same time?

As children develop the ability to see five as a subunit you may begin to see them count the number of groups of five. For example, they may say fifteen is three groups of five. Here they are unitizing; they are treating the five as a group, counted as one—one group of five.

❖ Commutativity and associativity

Algebraically, commutativity for addition is represented as a + b = b + a, and associativity for addition is represented as (a + b) + c = a + (b + c). Children need many opportunities to compose and decompose numbers before they come to realize that numbers can be grouped in a variety of ways, or presented in a different order, and the amounts stay the same.

❖ The relationship between addition and subtraction

As children gain flexibility in composing and decomposing numbers, they begin to generalize about the way in which the parts are related to the whole. One of the first generalizations they make is about how addition and subtraction are related. If 5 + 3 = 8, it necessarily follows that 8 − 3 must be 5. Algebraically stated, if a + b = c, then c − b = a.

STRATEGIES

As you work with the activities in this unit, you will notice that children use many strategies to derive combinations. Here are some strategies to notice:

- ❖ *using synchrony and one-to-one tagging*
- ❖ *counting three times*
- ❖ *counting on and counting back*
- ❖ *using the five- and ten-structures*
- ❖ *using trial and adjustment vs. systematic exploration*
- ❖ *using doubles and near doubles*
- ❖ *using compensation*
- ❖ *making ten*

❖ Using synchrony and one-to-one tagging

Counting effectively requires children to coordinate many actions simultaneously. Not only must they remember the word that comes next, they must use only one word for each object (synchrony) and tag each object once and only once (one-to-one tagging). Initially when children are learning to count, this coordination is very difficult; they often skip some objects, double-tag others, and are not synchronized, using too many or too few words for the number of objects they are counting.

❖ Counting three times

Making groups and determining the total number of objects in all the groups is also a huge undertaking. To determine the whole when adding the objects in two groups, children may tediously count three times—first each of the two groups and then the whole, starting from one each time. For example, to determine how many passengers are on the bus when 8 are on the lower deck and 9 are on the top deck, they may count 1 through 8, then 1 through 9, and then count from 1 all over again to 17.

❖ Counting on and counting back

A major landmark strategy to notice and celebrate is when a child begins to count on—labeling the first set 8, moving it to the side as a group, and then continuing with 9, 10, and on to 17. It is the developing understanding of the relationships of the parts and the whole that causes the shifts in the strategies. For subtraction, children also become able to count back until they reach the target amount, knowing that these amounts together make the whole.

❖ Using the five- and ten-structures

One of the most important ways of structuring number is to compose and decompose amounts into groups of five and ten. For example, seeing 8 as 5 + 3, or 7 as 5 + 2, is very helpful in automatizing the basic fact "8 + 7." Since 3 + 2 also equals 5, 8 + 7 is equivalent to 3 fives. The five-structure is also helpful in automatizing all the combinations that make ten— if 6 is equivalent to 5 + 1, then only 4 more are needed to make 2 fives, which equal 10. Similarly it can be helpful to think of 7 + 8 as 3 fives, or 9 + 7 as 10 + 6.

❖ Using trial and adjustment vs. systematic exploration

In exploring the number of passengers on the double-decker bus, children often begin to make arrangements of a given number of passengers using trial and error. They can't systematically generate all the possible arrangements of, say, eight passengers. But a major change to celebrate is when you see children beginning to use the results of their trials, and adjust the numbers. For example, to find different arrangements, they might try "plugging in numbers." They plug in a number of passengers on the upper deck and find out (for example, by adding one at a time or counting on) how many need to be on the lower deck to get to the total. They may use this information to generate another combination. As they find several that work, they will begin to generalize and their approach will become less random.

❖ Using doubles and near doubles

A great way to help children automatize the basic addition and subtraction facts is to work on relationships. For example, by itself 7 + 6 can be a difficult fact to learn but when it is explored in relation to a double such as 7 + 7 or 6 + 6 it is easier. Once the doubles are known, they can be used for many other problems: 5 + 7 = 6 + 6, 7 + 3 = 5 + 5, and 7 + 6 = 6 + 6 + 1 (or 7 + 7 − 1), etc.

❖ Using compensation

Once children understand compensation and equivalence, they use it to find all the combinations, and their approach becomes more systematic. They can easily reconfigure 5 + 8 as 4 + 9 and then as 3 + 10 as needed, to solve any particular problem.

❖ Making ten

Using the combinations of whole numbers that add up to ten is a powerful strategy that makes learning most of the more difficult basic facts easier. If children know that 8 + 2 is equivalent to 10, then it is quite easy for them to solve for 8 + 7. They simply take 2 from the 7 and give it to the 8. This produces 10 + 5.

MATHEMATICAL MODELING

The model developed in this unit is the arithmetic rack. Models go through three stages of development (Gravemeijer 1999; Fosnot and Dolk 2001):

❖ *model of the situation*

❖ *model of children's strategies*

❖ *model as a tool for thinking*

❖ Model of the situation

The arithmetic rack is introduced in this unit as a model of the situation of passengers on a double-decker bus. Just as the passengers on the bus can sit in various arrangements and go up and down the stairs from one deck to another, the beads on the arithmetic rack can reflect changes in the number of passengers on each deck.

❖ Model of children's strategies

Children benefit from seeing the teacher model their strategies. Once the model has been introduced as a representation of the situation, you can use it to model children's strategies as they determine arrangements of passengers on the bus. If a child counts by ones, move one bead at a time; if a child counts on, move the set, then move beads one at a time onto the set. If a child uses compensation, remove a bead from one group and slide another bead onto the other group.

❖ *Model as a tool for thinking*

Eventually children will be able to use this model as a tool for thinking—they will be able to imagine 6 + 4 reconfigured as 5 + 5 on the rack. Over time, the arithmetic rack can become an important model to support children in learning the basic facts for addition and subtraction (Treffers 1991).

Many opportunities to discuss these landmarks in mathematical development will arise as you work through the unit. Look for moments of puzzlement. Don't hesitate to let children discuss their ideas and check and recheck their counting. Celebrate their accomplishments! These are developmental milestones.

A graphic of the full landscape of learning for early number sense, addition, and subtraction is provided on page 10. The purpose of the graphic is to allow you to see the longer journey of children's mathematical development and to place your work with this unit within the scope of this long-term development. You may also find it helpful to use this graphic as a way to record the progress of individual children for yourself. Each landmark can be shaded in as you find evidence in a child's work and in what the child says—evidence that a big idea, strategy, or way of modeling has been constructed. In a sense, you will be recording the individual pathways children take as they develop as young mathematicians.

References and Resources

Dehaene, Stanislas. 1999. *The Number Sense: How the Mind Creates Mathematics.* New York, NY: Oxford University Press.

Dolk, Maarten, and Catherine Twomey Fosnot. 2004a. *Addition and Subtraction Minilessons, Grades PreK–3.* CD-ROM with accompanying facilitator's guide by Antonia Cameron, Sherrin B. Hersch, and Catherine Twomey Fosnot. Portsmouth, NH: Heinemann.

———. 2004b. *Fostering Children's Mathematical Development, Grades PreK–3: The Landscape of Learning.* CD-ROM with accompanying facilitator's guide by Sherrin B. Hersch, Antonia Cameron, and Catherine Twomey Fosnot. Portsmouth, NH: Heinemann.

Fosnot, Catherine Twomey, and Maarten Dolk. 2001. *Young Mathematicians at Work: Constructing Number Sense, Addition, and Subtraction.* Portsmouth, NH: Heinemann.

Gravemeijer, Koeno P. E. 1999. How emergent models may foster the constitution of formal mathematics. *Mathematical Thinking and Learning* 1 (2): 155–77.

Kamii, Constance. 1985. *Young Children Reinvent Arithmetic.* New York: Teachers College Press.

Treffers, Adri. 1991. *Rekenen tot twentig met het rekenrek* [Calculating to twenty with the arithmetic rack]. *Willem Bartjens* 10 (1): 35–45.

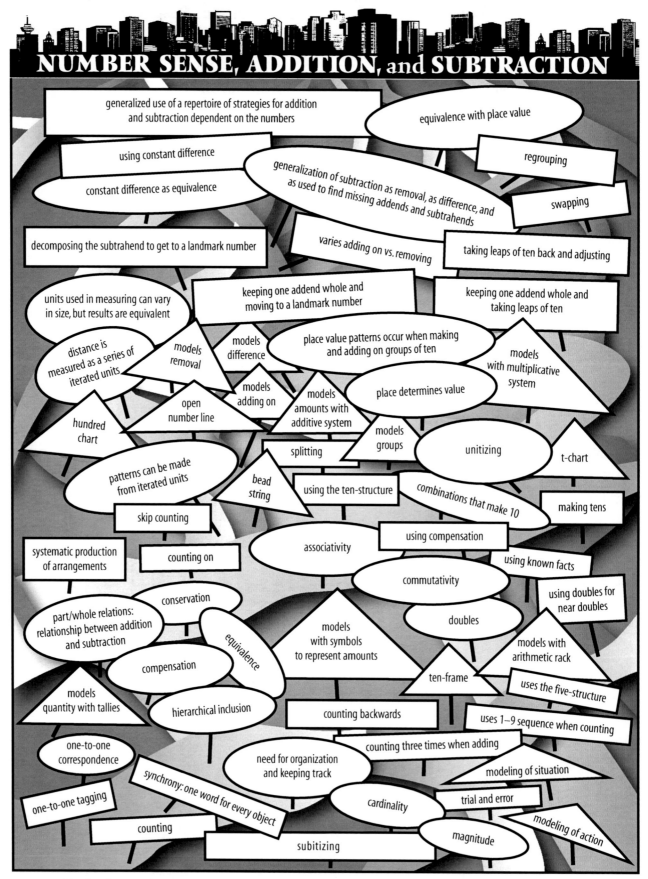

generalized use of a repertoire of strategies for addition and subtraction dependent on the numbers

equivalence with place value

using constant difference

regrouping

constant difference as equivalence

generalization of subtraction as removal, as difference, and as used to find missing addends and subtrahends

swapping

decomposing the subtrahend to get to a landmark number

varies adding on vs. removing

taking leaps of ten back and adjusting

units used in measuring can vary in size, but results are equivalent

keeping one addend whole and moving to a landmark number

keeping one addend whole and taking leaps of ten

distance is measured as a series of iterated units

models removal

models difference

place value patterns occur when making and adding on groups of ten

models with multiplicative system

open number line

models adding on

models amounts with additive system

place determines value

hundred chart

models groups

place value patterns

unitizing

t-chart

patterns can be made from iterated units

splitting

bead string

using the ten-structure

combinations that make 10

making tens

skip counting

using compensation

systematic production of arrangements

counting on

associativity

using known facts

commutativity

using doubles for near doubles

conservation

doubles

part/whole relations: relationship between addition and subtraction

equivalence

models with symbols to represent amounts

models with arithmetic rack

compensation

ten-frame

uses the five-structure

models quantity with tallies

hierarchical inclusion

counting backwards

uses 1–9 sequence when counting

one-to-one correspondence

counting three times when adding

modeling of situation

need for organization and keeping track

one-to-one tagging

synchrony: one word for every object

cardinality

trial and error

modeling of action

counting

magnitude

subitizing

The landscape of learning: number sense, addition, and subtraction on the horizon showing landmark strategies (rectangles), big ideas (ovals), and models (triangles).

The Double-Decker Bus

The story *The Double-Decker Bus* is used to introduce the arithmetic rack. After the children hear the story, the rack is displayed and they are encouraged to notice and make use of the five-structure. For example, 5 passengers on the upper deck of the bus and 8 on the lower deck are explored as a group of 5, another group of 5, and 3 more. The children then familiarize themselves with the arithmetic rack by recording various arrangements of passengers in seats on the bus.

Materials Needed

The Double-Decker Bus
[If you do not have the full-color read-aloud book (available from Heinemann), you can use Appendix A.]

Class-size arithmetic rack, with cover-up board

Individual arithmetic rack—one per pair of children

Instructions for making both types of arithmetic racks can be found in Appendix B. Visit contextsforlearning.com for information on where to purchase arithmetic racks.

Student recording sheet for bus passenger arrangements (Appendix C)—one per pair of children, with extras available

Day One Outline

Developing the Context

* Read *The Double-Decker Bus,* stopping periodically to discuss the number of passengers.

* Display the arithmetic rack and suggest that children think of the beads as bus passengers. Establish that there are 20 beads on the rack, arranged in groups of five.

* Show different bead arrangements designed to encourage children to use the five-structure of the rack.

* Have children explore additional bead arrangements and record their work in Appendix C.

Supporting the Investigation

* As children work with different bead arrangements, help them to notice and use the five-structure of the rack.

Preparing for the Math Congress

* Plan to scaffold a congress discussion that will help move children beyond counting by ones.

Facilitating the Math Congress

* Use the arithmetic rack to represent the strategies students share.

Developing the Context

- Read *The Double-Decker Bus,* stopping periodically to discuss the number of passengers.

- Display the arithmetic rack and suggest that children think of the beads as bus passengers. Establish that there are 20 beads on the rack, arranged in groups of five.

- Show different bead arrangements designed to encourage children to use the five-structure of the rack.

- Have children explore additional bead arrangements and record their work in Appendix C.

Read the story *The Double-Decker Bus* (Appendix A). Stop periodically to discuss the number of passengers on the bus. Be sure that children understand the context—that double-decker buses have two levels and that passengers can go up and down the stairs from one level to another. When you finish reading the story, display the class-size arithmetic rack. Explain that the rack has two decks just like the bus, and that the beads are in two colors to make it easier to figure out how many beads there are. Suggest that the children think of the beads as passengers in red and white seats and discuss how many there are on the bus, encouraging children to use the five-structure of the rack.

Once you establish the five-structure, explain that it is probably easier to tell how many passengers are on the bus when all the red seats are full. Have a discussion on the following situations:

- Use just the bottom row of the rack and show 5 red and 2 white beads. Ask the children if they think this arrangement would make it easy for the little girl in the story to determine the number of passengers.

- Then slide over 2 more white beads to display 9 beads on the bottom. Ask the children how the little girl might think about this one.

- Next, show 6 on the top and 9 on the bottom and ask, "What if the little girl sees this? Is there an easy way that she could figure out how many passengers there are, without counting everyone?"

- Finally, show 5 on the top and 8 on the bottom and ask, "What if she sees this?"

Behind the Numbers

On the bus in the story, there are exactly twenty seats, not including the driver's seat. Some children may need to touch each bead on the rack in order to count them; others may be comfortable counting the beads from a distance. The important thing is that children notice the five red beads and five white beads on each level of the rack.

Developing the Context

Inside One Classroom

Nina (the teacher): Let's pretend these beads are the passengers sitting in the seats—the ones the little girl can see through the windows. Let's pretend that the red beads show the passengers sitting in red seats, and the white beads show the passengers sitting in white seats. How many passengers can the little girl see?

Sophia: 1, 2, 3, 4, 5, 6, 7, 8, 9, 10, 11, 12, 13, 14, 15, 16, 17, 18, 19. It's 19.

Marie: Wait, I counted the beads too, and I got 20.

Nina: Can 19 and 20 both be right?

continued on next page

Author's Notes

Many children may need to count by ones to figure out how many people are on the bus. Some may even miss a bead, or count some twice. If this happens, have the children double-check each other's counts. Other children may be able to see small quantities as units and then count on. Some may use the colors and recognize that there are five red beads and five white beads in each row.

continued from previous page

Many voices: No.

Nina: Mary, come up here and count slowly. We'll count with you as you point to the beads. *(Mary points to each bead as she and the class count together.)* What do you think, Sophia?

Sophia: It's 20. I think I counted wrong before.

Jordan: 1, 2, 3, 4, 5, 6, 7, 8, 9, 10. There are 10 on the top and, uh, 10 on the bottom.

Jamal: Let me check—1, 2, 3, 4, and 5. The girl can see 5 people in the red seats on the bottom, and 5 in the white seats. It's the same on the top. So it's 10 and 10. That's 20!

Jamal comes up and physically touches the beads to check.

Nina: So you say there are 20 people on this bus. But you seem to see groups of 5. Can you say more about that, Jamal? That is an important thing to notice. I wonder if the little girl uses that idea. Would it help her to quickly see how many people are on the bus?

Nina emphasizes the use of the five-structure as she encourages Jamal to expand on his idea.

Once children have a good sense of how the colors and the five-structure can help them to quickly determine how many passengers are on the bus, assign partners. Distribute an individual arithmetic rack and a recording sheet (Appendix C) to each pair of children. (Have extra copies of the recording sheet on hand in case children need more). Explain that you want them to find a place in the room and take turns acting out being someone looking at the bus, like the little girl in the story. One child will be the bus driver and set up a bus situation with the beads on the rack, and the other child will try to find a fast way to figure it out before the bus drives away. You may want to role-play this scenario with a child to help the class understand what you want them to do. Have children record their findings as in Figure 1.

Behind the Numbers

The numbers here have been specifically chosen to support the use of the five-structure of the rack. Children are encouraged to see 7 beads as 5 and 2; 9 beads as 5 and 4, or as 10 minus 1; 6 plus 9 beads as three sets of five; and 5 plus 8 as 2 fives plus 3.

Figure 1

Author's Notes

Nina (the teacher): *(Showing 6 on the top and 9 on the bottom.)* How many passengers are riding the bus now? Can the little girl find this total in an easy way?

Max: 1, 2, 3, 4, 5, 6, and…7, 8, 9, 10, 11, 12, 13, 14, 15. It's 15.

Shanna: 1, 2, 3, 4, 5, 6. And 1, 2, 3, 4, 5, 6, 7, 8, 9. *(Pointing again at the passengers on the lower deck.)* Oh, wait, it's 7, 8, 9, 10, 11, 12, 13, 14, 15.

Jolie: No. I think she imagines one going down the stairs. *(Moving one bead on the top to the right and then one on the bottom to the left to make ten on the bottom.)* See, now there's 5 people on the top and 10 down here. Now it's easy—15 people.

Nina: Wow, that would be a fast way! Who can put in their own words what Jolie just did?

Some children will continue to count by ones. This is a reliable strategy for them, and they might need more experience with the arithmetic rack before they feel comfortable enough to rely on the group of five.

By moving some of the passengers, it is possible to create groups of five in a row.

Nina encourages paraphrasing of Jolie's strategy. Discussing each other's ideas builds community and helps everyone reflect on important ideas.

Supporting the Investigation

☀ As children work with different bead arrangements, help them to notice and use the five-structure of the rack.

As children work, move around the room supporting their investigation, and conferring with a few at a time. Expect to see various strategies:

+ Counting every bead, perhaps even missing some. As you confer with children who are still counting, support them in recording small groups, such as two, three, four, and particularly five.

+ Skip-counting by twos. Although this is a bit more efficient than counting by ones and you can celebrate it, also encourage these children to make use of the bead colors. Stay grounded in the context, reminding them that the little girl knew a lot about the buses. Ask if the colors of the seats (beads) might be even more helpful. Help them notice and use the five-structure.

+ Using doubles. You may not see many children making use of doubles today, since this is the first day of the unit, but as children become more accustomed to using the rack they will begin to use the two rows to make doubles—for example, 6 + 7 may be seen as 6 + 6 + 1.

▨ Assessment Tips

Notice which children count each bead to be sure—for example, that there are five people in the red or white seats or ten people on a deck. Note which counting strategies the children are using. Are they counting accurately? Are they counting on from small quantities? Which children use groups of five or ten? It is helpful to jot down your observations on sticky notes. These can be placed on children's recording sheets and included in their portfolios.

Conferring with Children at Work

Author's Notes

Jamal: I'm the bus driver. *(Showing 6 on top and 6 on the bottom.)*

Shanna: 5, 6, 7, 8, 9, 10, 11, 12.

Nina (the teacher)**:** That was really great, Shanna, the way you saw that 5 on the bottom all at once! I'm noticing that it's on the top too—5 red beads on the top and 5 red beads on the bottom.

Nina begins by observing the strategy that Shanna uses. Noticing that Shanna uses the five-structure as a subunit and counts on, Nina encourages her to use it on the top of the rack, too.

Shanna: That's 10!

Nina: Wow. That's a fast way! I bet you could tell how many passengers no matter how fast the bus is going! And then what about these people? *(Pointing to the two remaining.)*

Nina stays grounded in the context.

Shanna: 11, 12.

Nina: Having all the red ones full helps, doesn't it? Now you can write 5 + 5 + 2.

Restating helps Shanna and Jamal reflect on their actions.

Preparing for the Math Congress

When children have had a sufficient amount of time to work, ask them to think of one really helpful strategy for people to use in finding the total number of passengers as the bus goes by. They should be prepared to share their thinking in the math congress. As children discuss strategies with their partners, think about which ones you should highlight in the congress with the goal of supporting the mathematical development of your community.

☀ Plan to scaffold a congress discussion that will help move children beyond counting by ones.

Tips for Structuring the Math Congress

Look for strategies that will help move children beyond counting by ones. The congress will be brief, but it is important to encourage the children to reflect on the meaning of what they have been doing. Look for strategies where the children use a full group of five or a full group of ten and then add on from the five or ten, so they are not counting each bead. Also look for strategies where children use the empty seats instead of the seats with passengers—for instance, using the three empty seats to figure out that there are 17 passengers. Another strategy to look for is the use of doubles, combinations that children often know. For example, 7 and 6 passengers might be seen as 6 and 6 passengers and 1 more.

Facilitating the Math Congress

☀ Use the arithmetic rack to represent the strategies students share.

Invite one or two pairs of children to explain helpful strategies that allowed them to tell quickly how many passengers were on the bus without having to count. Use the class-size arithmetic rack during discussion to represent the strategies being shared.

Reflections on the Day

Today children were introduced to the arithmetic rack using the context of the double-decker bus. They became familiar with the five- and ten-structure of the arithmetic rack and developed strategies for figuring out how many passengers were riding the bus.

DAY TWO

How Many People Are on the Bus?

Today begins with a minilesson using quick images of passengers on the bus. Children revisit strategies discussed on Day One, investigate and construct different arrangements of passengers on the bus, and consider which arrangements are easy or difficult to recognize. The class then discusses these strategies in a math congress. A game, Passenger Pairs, is introduced as an opportunity for further use of these strategies.

Day Two Outline

Minilesson: Quick Images

☀ Show and discuss some quick image arrangements of beads on the arithmetic rack designed to encourage use of the five-structure.

Developing the Context

☀ Explore the situation of 8 passengers and ask the children to use their arithmetic racks to represent easy and difficult arrangements.

Supporting the Investigation

☀ Help children notice and use the five- and ten-structures of the rack.

Preparing for the Math Congress

☀ Plan to scaffold a congress discussion that will move from less efficient strategies to more efficient strategies.

Facilitating the Math Congress

☀ Have children use the arithmetic rack to model their thinking as they discuss easy and more difficult arrangements.

Developing the Context

☀ Model how to play Passenger Pairs.

Supporting the Investigation

☀ Look for evidence of children moving toward the use of the five-structure and other efficient strategies.

Materials Needed

The Double-Decker Bus (Appendix A)

Class-size arithmetic rack, with cover-up board

Individual arithmetic rack—one per pair of children

Student recording sheet for easy and hard arrangements (Appendix D)—one per pair of children

Passenger Pairs game cards (Appendix E)—one deck per pair of children

Rack Pairs game cards *(optional)* (Appendix F)—one deck per pair of children

Large chart pad and easel (or chalkboard or whiteboard)

Markers

Minilesson: Quick Images (10–15 minutes)

☀ Show and discuss some quick image arrangements of beads on the arithmetic rack designed to encourage use of the five-structure.

This minilesson uses a string of related quick images to support the use of the five-structure. Briefly display an arrangement of beads on the class-size arithmetic rack, and then cover it with the board or a piece of cloth. Give the children time to think about it, and then ask them to tell their neighbors the number of passengers on the bus and why they think that number is correct. Show the images long enough to allow children to see the groups of five but not long enough for them to count beads individually; this time constraint encourages children who are counting each passenger one at a time to shift to strategies that are more efficient. Invite a few children to share their strategies with the whole group. Record their thinking as equations and then move to the next quick image. (See Inside One Classroom, below, for an example of how this is done.)

Behind the Numbers

This is a beginning string of related problems to be shown on the arithmetic rack, to remind children of the five-structure and to encourage them to see it in various groupings of beads. The first image provides the structure that is used as the string progresses.

String of related quick images:

5 on the bottom

5 on the top, 5 on the bottom

6 on the bottom

8 on the bottom

7 on the bottom

10 on the top

A Portion of the Minilesson

Inside One Classroom

Author's Notes

Nina (the teacher): So here's the next one. *(Sliding over 8 on the bottom.)* I wonder if any of the other problems we have up here so far can be helpful. *(On the board is written 5 + 5 = 10; 5 + 1 = 6).*

Nina records the equations as she goes. The relationships between the problems can be helpful.

Carl: It's just 2 more. Before it was 5 and 1. Now it's 5 and 3.

Nina: That 5 is really helpful, isn't it? Nice noticing. Saves a lot of counting, doesn't it? How many altogether?

The children are encouraged to use the five-structure, but all strategies are accepted and discussed. Exploring a variety of strategies develops number sense.

Carl: There are 6, 7, 8. Eight.

Nina: *(Writes 8 = 5 + 3.)* Did anyone see 8 a different way?

Jordan: I did—2 more whites would be 10. So 10 minus 2.

Developing the Context

After the minilesson, assign math partners and distribute an individual arithmetic rack to each pair of children. Remind children of the double-decker bus story and their investigation on Day One—how they tried to find quick ways, like the girl in the story, to figure out how many passengers were on the bus before the bus pulled away. Recall that the same number of people can sit in different arrangements on the bus, some on the top deck and some on the bottom deck. Ask the children how the bus might look after eight people board. On the small racks, have the children arrange eight passengers and show different arrangements to each other. Ask them which arrangements would be easy for the girl to figure and which would be harder. What makes it easier to figure the total for some arrangements? What makes it harder to figure the total in others?

☀ Explore the situation of 8 passengers and ask the children to use their arithmetic racks to represent easy and difficult arrangements.

Assign each pair of children a particular number of passengers and ask each pair to arrange that number of passengers in two ways. One arrangement would make it really easy for the girl in the story to see how many passengers there are before the bus pulls away; another arrangement would make it more difficult. Ask the children to reflect on the following questions with their partners:

*   Why is it easy to figure the number in this arrangement?
*   Why is it hard to figure the number in this arrangement?

Do not ask the children to record pictures of their arrangements on paper. Making a drawing of their arrangement reinforces low-level counting strategies; instead, have the children use the recording sheet (Appendix D) to record only the numbers of passengers they see on the top deck and on the bottom deck (as in Figure 2). In the congress, you will have children show their arrangements on the arithmetic rack.

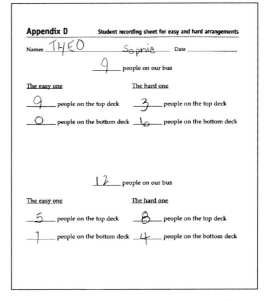

Figure 2

Differentiating Instruction

You can differentiate to provide appropriate challenges and support by the choice of numbers you assign. For children who are still counting each bead, assign numbers that are multiples or near multiples of five (for example, 15 or 9); for children who use groups of five or ten, you can assign more challenging numbers such as 13 or 17.

Behind the Numbers

In deciding easy or difficult arrangements of passengers, children who are still counting every bead might say that there is no real difference—after all, they have to count in each case. Children using groups of five and ten will find that it is easier to figure the number of passengers when the five-structure is apparent in the arrangement. Combinations like 4 on the upper deck and 8 on the lower deck might be considered difficult because no groups of five or ten stand out on their own—i.e., the one full group of five is nested within the 8.

Supporting the Investigation

☀ Help children notice and use the five- and ten-structures of the rack.

As you walk around, note the strategies children are using. Here are some strategies you might see:

✦ Counting each bead separately. Encourage these children to consider the group of five. Separate the beads by color and ask them to look just at the red ones. Move the red group as a unit and help them count on from it.

✦ Identifying a group of five and counting on: "Here's 5. So these beads are 6, 7, and 8." Here you can challenge children to record the subunits—8 as 5 and 3, 7 as 5 and 2, etc.

✦ Moving five beads as a group. As children begin to treat the five as a subunit, you can challenge them to consider how many groups of five they can make. Five on top and eight on the bottom, for example, would be seen as 2 fives and 3 ones. Counting the groups of five is unitizing—an important big idea on the landscape of early number sense.

✦ Using two groups of five passengers as a unit of ten. Encourage these children to use the ten-structure to figure out near-multiples of ten, such as 19 or 11.

Preparing for the Math Congress

☀ Plan to scaffold a congress discussion that will move from less efficient strategies to more efficient strategies.

After children have worked for a sufficient amount of time, remind them to record their easy and difficult arrangements on their recording sheets. Also, they should be prepared to discuss why they thought it was easy to figure one arrangement of passengers, and more difficult to figure the other arrangement.

▦ Tips for Structuring the Math Congress

You might scaffold the conversation in the congress by starting with children who count all the beads, one by one, then moving to children who are starting to group and find shortcuts, and ending with children who are using units of five and ten. Taking careful note of strategies that children have used will guide your decision about which children should share, and the order in which they should share. Try to anticipate the way that the conversation might flow and how the importance of using the five-structure will emerge in this conversation.

Facilitating the Math Congress

When you and the children are prepared to discuss seatings of passengers, ask all the children to bring their two arrangements with them as they convene in the meeting area. Ask them to sit next to their partners.

✦ Ask a pair of children who counted all the passengers one by one to share their arrangement of passengers on the class-size arithmetic rack. Ask, "How did you figure the total number of passengers?"

✦ Ask a pair who used the five- and ten-structures to share their easy combination. Ask them to share how they figured the number of passengers for that arrangement. Ask the other children if they could explain how this pair figured the number, and encourage some children who counted by ones to explain this strategy. Ask, "What makes this arrangement easy to count?"

✦ Have a group share an arrangement for which it's difficult to know the total number quickly. Discuss what makes this arrangement of beads more difficult to figure.

☀ Have children use the arithmetic rack to model their thinking as they discuss easy and more difficult arrangements.

A Portion of the Math Congress

Inside One Classroom

Nina (the teacher): Theo, can you tell us about the bus that you and Sophie worked on?

(Theo shows 9 passengers on the upper deck.)

Theo: See, there's 5 red and 4 white. I knew the reds, 5, and I counted on the white beads, 6, 7, 8, 9.

Jin: I think it's easy because I know there are 10 on the upper deck and there's 1 missing, so that's 9.

Nina: Jin says there's 1 missing on the top deck. How does he know that?

Mei: Well, there's 5 white beads and we see only 4, so one is hiding.

Nina: So, why is it an easy arrangement?

Sophie: Because you don't have to count. You can see the 5 and the 4 and that's 1 less than 5 and 5.

Author's Notes

Nina deliberately refrains from saying how many passengers are on the bus. This gives all the children an opportunity to think about it themselves.

Theo knows there are nine beads and explains how to check his work by counting on from the unit of five. Jin and Mei use what they know about the unit of ten on the arithmetic rack to figure the number of passengers.

Nina maximizes the math moment by encouraging children to examine nine as being the number that is one less than ten.

Developing the Context

☀ Model how to play Passenger Pairs.

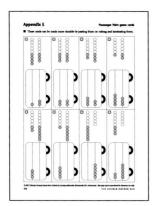

After the math congress, ask the children to form a circle. Choose a child to be your game partner as you introduce and model the Passenger Pairs game for the class.

▨ Object of the Game

The purpose of the game is to encourage children to examine different ways the same number of passengers can be seated and to explore why it is easier to recognize the totals in some arrangements than in others.

▨ Directions for Playing Passenger Pairs

The Passenger Pairs deck of game cards (Appendix E) includes 24 cards with different arrangements of bus passengers (twelve pairs of cards depicting the same number). Children play the game in pairs. They set up the game by mixing the cards and placing them, face up, in four rows of six. (The sun in the top right corner helps children orient the cards.) The children take turns finding two cards that depict the same number.

Player One picks up two cards, states the number they show and how the player knows, and asks Player Two for agreement or disagreement. If Player Two agrees that the two cards each show the same number of passengers, then the cards are placed on a discard pile. Then Player Two takes a turn selecting two matching cards. In all cases, the partners must agree whether the cards match. The matching pairs are placed in one discard pile, encouraging collaborative rather than competitive play.

Supporting the Investigation

☀ Look for evidence of children moving toward the use of the five-structure and other efficient strategies.

Assign math partners and have the children go to tables to play the game. Give each pair of children a deck of game cards. As children play, move around the room and sit with a few pairs. Children need time and experience to recognize a number on the arithmetic rack using groups of five and ten as part of the totals-recognition process. Passenger Pairs, which closely resembles the quick image activity in today's minilesson, encourages all the children to work and share ideas simultaneously. Listen in on the conversations between the children. Feel free to ask children how they know how many passengers there are. Some children may quickly figure the correct number of passengers but need help articulating their strategies. Here are questions that help children recognize their own mathematical thinking:

✦ Can you show on the cards how you got that number?

✦ Did you start from one, or did you start from another number?

Look for evidence of children moving toward the use of the five-structure and other efficient strategies. Note how children recognize cards with the same numbers. Do they count all one by one, use doubles and near doubles, or count on from groups of five and ten? Listen for evidence of mathematical thinking as children discuss their strategies.

Differentiating Instruction

There are two versions of this game: Passenger Pairs contains the easy set of cards (Appendix E), with 24 arrangements of passengers on a bus. Rack Pairs contains the difficult set (Appendix F), with 24 cards depicting beads on an arithmetic rack. In Rack Pairs, the context of the double-decker bus is implicit rather than explicit, and the arrangements of numbers of beads make recognition of the totals shown on each card more difficult to figure as well. Children who easily recognize the totals depicted on the Passenger Pairs cards should be encouraged to try Rack Pairs.

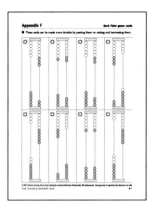

Reflections on the Day

Today children had several opportunities to explore how numbers of beads that are equivalent can be arranged differently. They reflected on using groups of five and ten to easily recognize total numbers; and in the math congress they were encouraged to use groups of five and ten systematically.

Moving between the Decks

Materials Needed

The Double-Decker Bus
(Appendix A)

Class-size arithmetic rack, with cover-up board

Individual arithmetic rack—one per child

Quick images
(Appendix G)

Drawing paper—at least one sheet per pair of children

Large chart pad and easel

Markers

After starting off with a few quick images, children investigate all possible ways of arranging a fixed number of passengers into two possible locations. How many different placements do they think of? How do they know if they have listed all the possibilities? What strategies help them organize and think up new placements? The children will reflect on and revise their work and then discuss their ideas in a math congress. The big ideas that emerge from this investigation are compensation and equivalence—understanding that moving passengers from one deck to the other deck does not change the total number of passengers.

Day Three Outline

Minilesson: Quick Images

☀ Show and discuss some quick image arrangements of beads on the arithmetic rack designed to encourage use of the five-structure.

Developing the Context

☀ Have children use their arithmetic racks to model different scenarios of passengers moving from one deck of the bus to the other.

☀ Assign a number of passengers to each pair of children and have them figure out all the possible configurations for that number of passengers.

Supporting the Investigation

☀ Note children's strategies as they explore different arrangements of passengers.

Preparing for the Math Congress

☀ Consider highlighting the work of children who verged on using a systematic approach to finding all possible arrangements.

Facilitating the Math Congress

☀ Encourage children to figure out ways to be certain that all possible arrangements have been found.

Minilesson: Quick Images (10–15 minutes)

Start with two or three quick images on the class-size arithmetic rack (more possible combinations are suggested in Appendix G). Show the image long enough to allow children to see the groups of five but not long enough to count each bead. After giving them a few moments to think, ask them to tell their neighbor how many beads they saw and how they know that this number is correct.

☀ Show and discuss some quick image arrangements of beads on the arithmetic rack designed to encourage use of the five-structure.

> **String of related quick images:**
>
> **10 on the top, 9 on the bottom**
>
> **8 on the top, 10 on the bottom**
>
> **9 on the top, 9 on the bottom**

A Portion of the Minilesson

Inside One Classroom

Nina (the teacher): Here we go. Ready and…look! What did you see?

Jamal: I saw 17.

Nina: How did you see 17?

Jamal: I saw 10 on top and 5 and 2 more on the bottom.

Marita: I saw 17 too. I saw 5 reds and another group of 5 reds—that's 10—and a group of 5 whites. That's 15. Then I counted, 16, 17.

Juan: My way was different. I noticed there's 3 missing. If they were all there it would be 20. And 20 minus 3 is 17.

Mei: Oh…I thought I saw 16. I saw the 10 and the 5 and I counted 15, 16. Wait, 15 and 1 more is 16, and then 1 more is 17.

Author's Notes

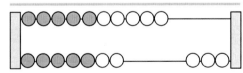

Counting each bead in this image is nearly impossible in a few seconds. This constraint pushes children who count one bead at a time to find other strategies. Those who tried counting each bead and had no time to finish should be encouraged to describe and try another child's strategy.

Children who are new at using the five- or ten-structure often make mistakes, miscounting the remaining beads. When this happens, the discussion can focus on what's left after isolating the five- or ten-structure and how those beads can be counted.

Developing the Context

☀ Have children use their arithmetic racks to model different scenarios of passengers moving from one deck of the bus to the other.

☀ Assign a number of passengers to each pair of children and have them figure out all the possible configurations for that number of passengers.

Remind children of the double-decker bus story, in which the wind and rain sent passengers from the upper to the lower deck. Consider that the reverse might also happen: that if the weather got warmer or sunnier, passengers might be tempted to go from the lower deck to the upper. This sets the stage for the introduction of the ideas of compensation and equivalence—that rearranging objects between two groups will not change the total number of objects.

Ask children to show, on the individual arithmetic racks, 5 passengers on the upper deck and 7 on the lower deck. Have the children use their racks to show what happens when a passenger goes downstairs. Ask, "Who can explain what happens to the total number of passengers?" These ideas should emerge:

- One number decreases from 5 to 4, while the other number increases from 7 to 8.

- The total number of passengers, 12, does not change.

Ask children to predict what these numbers would be if another passenger goes downstairs. What would the numbers be if yet another passenger goes downstairs? What would the numbers be if 2 or 3 passengers move between decks? Check predictions on the class-size arithmetic rack, and use numerals to record your findings. For example, write on the board:

5 on the top, 8 on the bottom

6 on the top, 7 on the bottom

7 on the top, 6 on the bottom

Ask the children if they notice any patterns in the numerals and why the patterns occur. Ask if they think these are all the possible combinations.

Behind the Numbers

In this investigation, children are asked to find (and list on paper) all possible ways a number of passengers can be split between the upper and lower decks. Allow children to organize their ideas in their own way; do not try to organize or systematize their work too early in the investigation. In this context, the emphasis is on compensation and equivalence. Using numerals instead of drawings of beads to record the number of people on the upper and lower decks will help children move away from counting each bead one by one.

Assign math partners and ask children to explore other possible numbers of passengers going up and down because of the rain or the sun. Assign a number of passengers to each pair of children, and have them figure out all the possible configurations for that number of passengers. What are all the possible numbers of passengers on the upper and lower decks? The children's work is to list as many of these combinations as possible. Provide them with drawing paper to record their findings. For this scenario, only the total number of passengers on each deck is important. The choice of numbers you make allows you to differentiate, but it is also important to give the same number to several pairs of children. Doing so will allow children to compare their findings during the math congress.

Supporting the Investigation

Walk around and listen as children discuss their thinking. Note what strategies they use. You might see children use one or more of the following strategies. Do they:

☀ Note children's strategies as they explore different arrangements of passengers.

+ use a guess-and-check approach?

+ plug in a random number (e.g., the passengers on the top deck), and figure out how many more are needed to reach the total?

+ conclude that they have all possible combinations because they can't think of any more?

+ use compensation systematically, by moving passengers between decks one at a time?

+ use the commutative property? For instance, if 8 are on the upper deck and 5 on the lower deck; then another possibility is 5 on the upper deck and 8 on the lower deck.

Children can use several different strategies to find different combinations. One strategy is "plugging in numbers." They plug in a number of passengers on the upper deck and find out (for example, by adding one at a time or counting on) how many need to be on the lower deck to get to the assigned total. Using compensation is another strategy. They might start with a number of passengers on the upper deck and move them down one by one. Some children may realize that when you start with all passengers on the upper deck, you will find all possible combinations. Using the commutative property of addition is another possible strategy. Children often call this "using opposites," "turnarounds" or "switches." If 3 passengers on the upper deck and 6 on the lower deck is a combination that adds up to the assigned total, then 6 on the upper and 3 on the lower is another combination. Children might use several strategies at one time. They might start by plugging in a random number, realize they can use opposites to find a second combination, use compensation to find a new combination, and continue. This switching between strategies, while eliciting different combinations, makes it confusing and difficult to know if all possible combinations have been identified.

Conferring with Children at Work

Inside One Classroom

Author's Notes

Jordan: We have 13 passengers. We could put 3 on the top and 10 on the bottom.

Nina begins by just listening. The best conferences begin with children's ideas.

Shanna: Yeah. Hey, then we could put 10 on the top and 3 on the bottom.

Nina (the teacher)**:** That's interesting, Shanna. How did you come up with that one so fast?

continued on next page

continued from previous page

Shanna: You can just switch 'em. It'll be the same.

Nina: Really? Will that always work?

Shanna: Yeah. See, it's still 13—10 and 3, just switched.

By questioning Shanna, Nina confirms that she is using the commutative property for addition, and challenges her to generalize.

Nina: Using shortcuts like that will help you find a lot of ways. I wonder if there are other shortcuts to find lots of ways. If one person comes down the stairs, is the amount still the same too? What if two come down?

Shanna: Yeah, that's a good way, too.

Wondering aloud is a great way to invite others to consider an idea. Here Nina encourages the children to consider compensation.

Preparing for the Math Congress

☀ Consider highlighting the work of children who verged on using a systematic approach to finding all possible arrangements.

When selecting student work to discuss during the math congress, consider children who verged on using a systematic approach, such as opposites (the commutative property) or compensation. Sharing their work might help them articulate their strategy and provide an opportunity for other children to build on their thinking.

Facilitating the Math Congress

☀ Encourage children to figure out ways to be certain that all possible arrangements have been found.

Convene the children in the meeting area to discuss the combinations they found. Have them sit next to their partners with their drawing paper. Ask two or three pairs of children to share strategies they found helpful and explain why they were helpful. During the conversation, pose the following questions:

✦ Can we use this idea to come up with more combinations?

✦ Will this strategy help us find all the arrangements that are possible?

✦ How do we know for certain that we have them all?

A Portion of the Math Congress

Author's Notes

Nina (the teacher): How do we know if we found all of the ways? Suzanne, I heard you say something interesting about this. Can you share what you and Jolie were discussing?

Suzanne: We tried different ways of putting 17 people on the bus. We started with 10 people on the top—that's when all the seats are full. Then you asked us if we had all the ways. We couldn't think of any more so we thought we had all of them, but now I think you can do more. *(Their list systematically shows:*

10 top, 7 bottom
9 top, 8 bottom
8 top, 9 bottom, etc.,
until they reach
1 top, 16 bottom)

Jolie: Look, there's a pattern.

Nina: Can you tell us more about the last situation, 1 on top and 16 on the bottom. I know you two talked for a long time about that one.

Suzanne: We know that only 10 people can be on one deck. But we said that some of these combinations could happen if people stood up.

Nina: Jolie said there is a pattern. What does she mean?

Carl: Those numbers are going down. The other numbers are going up.

Suzanne: We kept having one person go down the stairs. That's how we got the pattern.

Nina: What do you think of Suzanne and Jolie's strategy? Is it a good strategy?

Max: Yeah, but why did you start with those numbers?

Suzanne: We knew 10 and 7 was 17.

Nina: Why didn't they find all the combinations? What would you suggest they do next time so they could find all the different ways?

Nina allows Suzanne to explain their strategy and show all the combinations they found. She knows their strategy is powerful but there are still some combinations missing. This dialogue gives all the children an opportunity to discuss both the list of combinations and the strategy.

Suzanne is still talking about the bus context, even when her solution doesn't fit the context anymore. She and Jolie have started to move away from the strict context of the bus seats and have started investigating the mathematics in the situation.

Not finding all the combinations does not mean that this strategy is not powerful. For Suzanne and Jolie, the strategy is very effective even though they did not make use of the best starting place. Nina encourages discussion of the strategy and an examination of the pattern that Jolie sees.

Nina returns to an examination of the strategy. Implicitly she is developing the idea of what makes a good question in this community of young mathematicians at work. What do we think of this strategy? Is it helpful in cases like this? Why are they missing some combinations? How could the strategy be refined?

Reflections on the Day

Today children had the opportunity to explore equivalent combinations of passengers on a bus. In the bus context and with the support of the visual model provided by the arithmetic rack, children could imagine a passenger physically going up or down between decks. Depending on ideas and strategies that emerged, the activity allowed them to build understanding of equivalence and compensation.

DAY FOUR

Choice Day

Materials Needed

Class-size arithmetic rack, with cover-up board

Quick images (Appendix G)

Passenger Pairs game cards from Day Two—one deck per pair of children

Rack Pairs game cards (Appendix F)—one deck per pair of children

Blank Passenger Pairs game cards (Appendix H)—several per pair of children

Blank Rack Pairs game cards (Appendix I)—several per pair of children

Today the math workshop begins again with strings of related quick images that further develop ideas that were emerging on Day Three. Children then play several games that build on strategies they have constructed and explored in the last few days. The games also provide for differentiation and consolidation.

Day Four Outline

Minilesson: Quick Images

* Show and discuss some quick image arrangements of beads on the arithmetic rack designed to reinforce and build on ideas that emerged in the math congress on Day Three.

* Encourage children to notice patterns in the answers.

Choice Time

* Help children choose a game that will best support their strategy development.

Minilesson: Quick Images (10–15 minutes)

Show and discuss a few quick image arrangements of beads on the arithmetic rack. The following sequences support the ideas that are likely to have emerged during discussions on Day Three. Two strings of problems are provided. (Some more are listed in Appendix G). Choose a string that will reinforce and build on ideas that emerged in the math congress on Day Three. Depending on how much time you have, you can also do both.

※ Show and discuss some quick image arrangements of beads on the arithmetic rack designed to reinforce and build on ideas that emerged in the math congress on Day Three.

※ Encourage children to notice patterns in the answers.

String of related quick images #1:

    7 on the top, 3 on the bottom

    6 on the top, 4 on the bottom

    5 on the top, 5 on the bottom

    8 on the top, 4 on the bottom

String of related quick images #2:

    6 on the top, 3 on the bottom

    3 on the top, 6 on the bottom

    5 on the top, 8 on the bottom

    8 on the top, 5 on the bottom

    7 on the top, 3 on the bottom

    3 on the top, 7 on the bottom

Behind the Numbers

The images shown in the first string support the development of compensation. The first three problems all have the same answer and are illustrative of just one passenger going up or down. The last image challenges children to start with a ten $(8 + 2)$ and add 2. It can also become a double $(6 + 6)$ when using compensation.

The images shown in the second string support the development of the commutative property of addition. The string consists of three pairs. The problems in each pair result in the same total number of upper deck plus lower deck passengers. As you proceed through the string, no matter what strategies children are using, the pattern in the answers will become apparent and the "switching" can be discussed. For instance, as children start to remark that the total of passengers is the same, you can ask them to explain how they knew so quickly. You can also ask if the total always remains the same if the numbers of upper- and lower-deck passengers are switched.

Choice Time

Children can choose from the following games:

※ Help children choose a game that will best support their strategy development.

+ Passenger Pairs (the easy Pairs game)

+ Rack Pairs (the difficult Pairs game)

+ Passenger Combos (for this game you will need the deck of cards from Passenger Pairs or Rack Pairs as well as the corresponding blank cards from Appendix H or I)

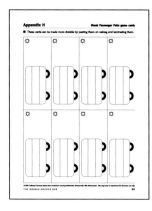

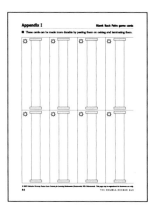

Passenger Pairs and Rack Pairs

Playing these games helps children to recognize number images, and encourages them to consider different ways that the same number of passengers can be seated. These games are described on pages 22–23.

Passenger Combos

Lay out, face up, all the cards from either the Passenger Pairs or Rack Pairs deck. Working in pairs, children sort the cards into stacks so that each stack contains all the cards showing the same number of passengers, even though the arrangements are different. (The sun in the top right corner helps children orient the cards.) When all the cards have been sorted into stacks, children examine the stacks to see if there could be other cards that would belong in that stack. Using the blank cards in either Appendix H or I, the children create the missing cards in order to have complete sets of cards showing possible combinations of whole numbers that add up to the same total.

Differentiating Instruction

There are two decks of cards with number combinations. Passenger Pairs contains the easy set, with 24 arrangements of passengers on a bus. Rack Pairs contains the difficult set, with 24 cards depicting beads on an arithmetic rack. Passenger Combos is more difficult than the original Passenger Pairs and Rack Pairs games, since it requires children to generate the missing arrangements. It also pushes the development of the compensation strategy and the commutative property of addition. The two sets of cards and two possible games per set allow for four different possibilities as you consider differentiation.

Reflections on the Day

Today children played games that supported them in recognizing number combinations using five- and ten-structures quickly, recognizing amounts that are equivalent but in different configurations. The construction of missing cards in Passenger Combos promoted using compensation to find all combinations of specific numbers.

DAY FIVE

Combinations of Ten

Children revisit the bus story to explore combinations of whole numbers that sum to ten. They think about the number of filled and empty seats on each deck and share ways to figure out how one number can be used to determine the other number. Using numbers that encourage counting on and counting back, the children have an opportunity to notice and discuss the relationship between addition and subtraction.

Day Five Outline

Developing the Context

☀ Read an excerpt from *The Double-Decker Bus.*

☀ Use the arithmetic rack to show some seating arrangements and discuss ways to find out the number of empty seats on the top deck without counting each one.

☀ Ask children to work on the problems in Appendix J.

Supporting the Investigation

☀ Note children's strategies as they determine the number of empty seats remaining on the top deck.

Preparing for the Math Congress

☀ Plan to scaffold a congress discussion to support children in learning the addition facts that make ten.

Facilitating the Math Congress

☀ Discuss and record children's strategies.

☀ Display an arrangement of beads on the arithmetic rack and have children apply the strategies they have shared.

Minilesson: Quick Images

☀ Show and discuss some quick image arrangements of beads on the arithmetic rack designed to highlight the strategies of counting on and counting back.

Materials Needed

The Double-Decker Bus (Appendix A)

Class-size arithmetic rack, with cover-up board

Individual arithmetic rack—one per pair of children

Student recording sheet for making tens (Appendix J)—one per pair of children

Large chart pad and easel

Markers

Developing the Context

☀ Read an excerpt from *The Double-Decker Bus*.

☀ Use the arithmetic rack to show some seating arrangements and discuss ways to find out the number of empty seats on the top deck without counting each one.

☀ Ask children to work on the problems in Appendix J.

Remind the children of *The Double-Decker Bus* and read the following excerpt:

I like it when Daddy tells me about the buses. "Sometimes," he says, "when people get on the bus, they ask if there are any seats on the upper deck. But I can't tell them because I can't see up there." I helped him figure it out. I told him if he knew how many people were on the bus altogether, he could just subtract the people he could see on the bottom. Then he would know how many were on the top. He liked my idea and he tried it. That night, when Daddy came home from work, he told me the idea had worked!

"This morning," he explained, "I knew that eight passengers had boarded the bus. And I saw just two of them sitting behind me downstairs. So I figured that there must be six sitting upstairs. I know there are ten seats upstairs, so I was able to tell a lady who asked that there were four empty seats on top."

Ask children if they can paraphrase the girl's thinking. Could they explain to the bus driver an easy way to find out the number of empty seats on the top deck without counting each one? Use the class-size arithmetic rack to show some seating arrangements and discuss ways to find out how many empty seats there are on the upper deck of each bus without going up to count.

Assign math partners and distribute an individual arithmetic rack and a recording sheet (Appendix J) to each pair of children. For each picture on the page, ask the children to investigate how many empty seats there are on the lower deck and on the upper deck. Ask children to explain a strategy that would help the bus driver figure out how many empty seats there are on the top without going up to count them.

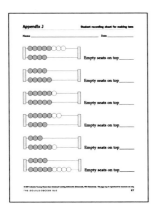

Supporting the Investigation

☀ Note children's strategies as they determine the number of empty seats remaining on the top deck.

As children work, walk around the room and observe the strategies they are discussing. Sit with a few pairs of children and confer. Determining the empty seats remaining on the upper deck without counting actually requires that children investigate number combinations that make ten. They might come up with several solutions. For instance, they can add on from the number of passengers on the upper deck using the five-structure to reach ten. They can also count back from ten to the number of passengers.

Conferring with Children at Work

Author's Notes

Marita and Juan are exploring a bus with 9 passengers. 6 are on the bottom deck so they know 3 have gone to the top deck.

Marita: If the 6 down here go up top, it's 9 seats that are full.

Juan: Yep, now the 6 on the bottom are empty and there is 1 more empty on the top. So there must have been 7 empty seats.

Nina (the teacher)**:** How would the bus driver know that if he can't see up top and the passengers don't go up there?

Juan: (Looking puzzled.) I don't know.

Nina: At first there were 3 up there, right? Would it help to think of them all sitting on the red side?

Juan: Then there's 2 more empty red ones.

Marita: And nobody's in the white seats.

Nina: So the white ones are empty? How many empty seats is that— 2 red ones and 5 white ones?

Marita: It's 7.

Juan: Hey, that's a good way to help him. He could make the people sit in the red seats first.

Nina: Or maybe he could just imagine them sitting there. Then he could let them sit where they wanted but he could think about them sitting in the red seats. Try your idea out on this next one…4 on the top deck and 9 on the bottom.

Nina begins conferring by listening. She notes that while Marita and Juan use the strategy of filling the top deck, they are simply modeling the action of the passengers going up and filling the seats. She brings the arrangement back to the starting position (three on top, six on the bottom). She now challenges them to think from the bus driver's perspective.

Juan begins to use the five-structure. Nina supports the use of this strategy by paraphrasing what they are doing.

The conference ends with a challenge.

Preparing for the Math Congress

In preparation for the math congress, ask the children to think of what they would tell the bus driver—a strategy he could use to figure out the number of empty seats on the top deck, even though he can't see them. Explain that at the math congress a few children will have a chance to teach the bus driver what to do, and that you will play the role of the bus driver. Have them put their recording sheets in their work folders. They will not need them in the congress.

☀ Plan to scaffold a congress discussion to support children in learning the addition facts that make ten.

▨ Tips for Structuring the Math Congress

Select two or three pairs of children who will offer interesting strategies, such as using all of the red seats first (using the five-structure) and counting on to ten, or subtracting the number of seats on the top from ten, or counting back from ten. The strategies you choose will be the focus of conversation in the congress, and should help to support children in learning the addition facts that make ten.

Facilitating the Math Congress

☀ Discuss and record children's strategies.

☀ Display an arrangement of beads on the arithmetic rack and have children apply the strategies they have shared.

Convene the children in the meeting area to discuss the strategies they found. It is not necessary, but it might be fun for you to wear a bus driver's hat (if you can find one). Have two or three children (one at a time) explain to you, the bus driver, what you should do to figure out how many empty seats there are on the top deck. Write down what they say on a large piece of chart paper, making a list of the different strategies the children developed. Use the class-size arithmetic rack to show a bus with 4 passengers on the upper deck and 6 on the lower deck. Ask the children to discuss how the different strategies would work in this situation. Have them help you use the strategies on the list.

Inside One Classroom

A Portion of the Math Congress

Author's Notes

Nina (the teacher): OK, so you've explained several things I could do to figure out the number of empty seats on top. I'll show you a bus. Let's see if each of these strategies works. (Uses class-size arithmetic rack with 4 beads on the top and 6 on the bottom). Help me use your strategy, Juan.

Juan: Make everybody on top sit in the red seats. There are 4 people so you need 1 seat to fill the reds. Then think of the whites. There's 5, so that's 6.

Nina: I'm not sure where you got the 1 and the 5. Can someone else explain where Juan got the 1 and 5?

Nina feigns ignorance to encourage everyone to consider how Juan has made use of the five-structure. Using the five-structure will be very helpful in helping to automatize the basic facts that make ten.

Suzanne: There are 4 people on the top. So 1 more makes 5, the 5 reds. The white seats are still empty. That's the 5.

Mei: Do it Jordan's way. They're sort of the same. He says to start at 10. That's the number of seats up top. He goes back 4. I know 4 + 1 is 5 and 5 extra is 10. But that sounds like "making five."

Nina: Who can help me? Is Jordan's way different?

Jamal: A little bit the same and a little bit different. Jordan subtracted, we added.

Nina: Are you saying that I can use either subtraction or addition to find the number of empty seats?

When children count backward, they sometimes get confused about what the numbers mean. Here they simultaneously need to track both the number of occupied seats and the number of empty seats.

The relationship between addition and subtraction is a big idea that children need to develop. Jordan's way—start at ten and subtract the number of passengers—is compared to the strategy of adding on. By choosing to share Jordan's and Juan's strategies in the congress, Nina knows it is more likely that children will start comparing the two approaches.

THE DOUBLE-DECKER BUS

Minilesson: Quick Images (10–15 minutes)

Now that children have discussed several strategies for finding the missing amounts, they can try them out. On the class-size arithmetic rack, show only numbers on the top. Show the image briefly—long enough for the children to see the beads but not long enough for counting each individual bead. For each image, ask, "How many beads on the top are missing?" Let the children discuss how they figured the number needed to make a sum of ten. There is a nice opportunity here for children to notice and compare numbers for which it is easier to count on and those for which it is easier to count back.

☀ Show and discuss some quick image arrangements of beads on the arithmetic rack.

String of related quick images:

3 on the top

7 on the top

2 on the top

8 on the top

6 on the top

Behind the Numbers

The first four problems are paired to accentuate the relationship between addition and subtraction and to support children in using either counting on or counting back strategies but with the five-structure as an image. The last problem has no pair, requiring children to think of it on their own.

Reflections on the Day

Today, the children explored combinations that make ten, using first the context of passengers on the bus and then simply the arithmetic rack. They shared strategies, which might have included counting on, counting back, and using groups of five in either direction. They may also have noticed and discussed the important relationship between addition and subtraction.

DAY SIX
Addition on the Arithmetic Rack

Materials Needed

Class-size arithmetic rack, with cover-up board

Individual arithmetic rack—one per child

Bus Stop game cards (addition) (Appendix L)—one deck per group of two or three children

Blank Bus Stop game cards (optional) (Appendix K)

Large chart pad and easel

Markers

Today the children will investigate the story context of people getting on the bus at various bus stops—addition situations. Several situations will be acted out using the arithmetic rack to support the development of addition strategies. An addition game, Bus Stop, is then introduced to further promote fluency with addition.

Day Six Outline

Minilesson: Quick Images

☀ Show and discuss some quick image arrangements of beads on the arithmetic rack designed to focus on the combinations of two whole numbers that sum to ten.

Developing the Context

☀ Present two bus scenarios focused on addition, and have children use their arithmetic racks to represent the situations.

☀ Model how to play Bus Stop.

Supporting the Investigation

☀ Note the addition strategies children use as they play the game.

Preparing for the Math Congress

☀ Plan for a congress discussion that will highlight the strategies children found most helpful as they played the game.

Facilitating the Math Congress

☀ Present a new bus stop problem and ask the children to use their arithmetic racks to solve it.

☀ As children share their strategies, use the arithmetic rack to model their thinking.

Minilesson: Quick Images (10–15 minutes)

The combinations of two whole numbers that sum to ten are the focus of this minilesson. Show the images briefly on the class-size arithmetic rack and invite solutions and explanations. Do one quick image at a time and ask how many passengers are on board. Explore a variety of strategies that children offer.

☀ Show and discuss some quick image arrangements of beads on the arithmetic rack designed to focus on the combinations of two whole numbers that sum to ten.

> **String of related quick images:**
>
> **8 on the top, 0 on the bottom**
>
> **7 on the top, 3 on the bottom**
>
> **4 on the top, 6 on the bottom**
>
> **6 on the top, 4 on the bottom**
>
> **9 on the top, 2 on the bottom**
>
> **8 on the top, 3 on the bottom**

Behind the Numbers

The first problem encourages counting on to fill the deck, because eight is so close to ten. The second problem may encourage compensation. One is lost on top but gained down below. The next pair may bring up a conversation on the commutative property, allowing you to revisit that idea, and the last two problems are easily solved if children use a combination that makes ten.

Developing the Context

Remind the children that the bus driver in the story wanted to keep track of the number of passengers on the bus so he would know how many empty seats there were on the top deck. Have them think about the following scenario:

☀ Present two bus scenarios focused on addition, and have children use their arithmetic racks to represent the situations.

☀ Model how to play Bus Stop.

> *One morning, a bus driver started a bus route and twelve passengers got on the double-decker bus. The bus driver knew that because he saw six going to the upper deck and six to the lower deck. At the second stop, four more people came on the bus. He wondered how many passengers were now on the bus.*

Have the children use their individual arithmetic racks to model the situation. Ask questions like "How can you show that on the arithmetic rack?" Record several combinations, asking "How do you know that it is sixteen? What is an easy way to tell?"

Continue the bus story with a second scenario:

> *He made several more stops and people got on and some got off the bus. Later in the day, he noticed that there were seven passengers on the bus and at the next stop five people got on.*

Ask children to use their racks and then share with the person sitting next to them how they know how many passengers are on the bus. Use a blank Bus Stop game card (Appendix K), or make a large drawing of it if the card is too small for all the children to see. Write "7" in the bus on the card and explain that the bus shows the number of passengers on the bus. Write "+5" in the bus stop sign and explain that this number shows what happened at the bus stop. Tell them that these cards will tell bus stories in a new game they will learn.

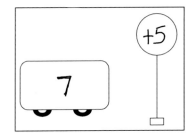

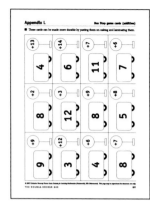

▨ Object of the Game

The purpose of the game is to encourage children to examine a variety of ways that the same number of passengers can be seated and to explore how some arrangements of passengers are easier than others to recognize and that these can be very helpful when adding.

▨ Directions for Playing Bus Stop

The game is played in groups of two or three. Give each player an individual arithmetic rack and each group a deck of addition Bus Stop game cards (Appendix L), face down in a stack. The number in the bus image tells how many passengers are on the bus as it approaches a bus stop. The round signs indicate the number of people at the bus stop, ready to enter the bus.

Player One turns over a card. All players show the bus scenario on their racks, discuss how many passengers are on the bus as it drives away, and compare how they used the beads to show their thinking. Player Two turns over a card and, again, all players show and compare arrangements on their racks. Players continue taking turns until the cards are used up.

Supporting the Investigation

☀ Note the addition strategies children use as they play the game.

As children play the game, move around and listen to the strategies they use for addition. Note how they are arranging the beads on the racks. Confer and support their investigation as needed.

Differentiating Instruction

Different number combinations suggest different ways to distribute the numbers on the top and bottom of the arithmetic rack. Talk with children about how knowing both numbers might influence a good setup of the first number. Children can investigate different ways to show the same situation of adding new passengers on the rack, and discuss which combinations make the numbers easier to add.

Use the blank Bus Stop game cards (Appendix K) to make more game cards as needed, or to make game cards with appropriate numbers for the children in your class.

▨ Assessment Tips

Listen in on children's conversations and observe what strategies they use. Do they use a making ten strategy, compensation, doubles, or near doubles? Use the landscape of learning graphic on page 10 as a way to record individual pathways representative of children's growth and development. You might find it helpful to make copies of the graphic, one for each child, and record growth and pathways by shading in the landmarks as children pass them.

Conferring with Children at Work

Sophia: Ah, 9 and 9. There's 9 people on the bus and 9 at the stop. This is an easy one; I know 9 + 9 is 18.

Suzanne: Yeah, adding 9 is like adding 10, only you do too much, so you have to take away one—9 + 10 = 19.

Nina (the teacher)**:** That's a neat strategy, Suzanne. Do you use that strategy other times, too?

Suzanne: Yep. Like for 19. You could add 20 and take 1 away.

Jamal: Next one—8 passengers on board and 5 at the bus stop. Oh, that's not so easy. Well, 8 on top, 5 on the bottom. Oh, 5 + 5 = 10, and 3 more makes 13. That *was* easy.

Nina: Suzanne, would your 9 strategy be helpful here? Could we use it for 8?

Suzanne: *(Looks a bit puzzled and then looks at the rack where she has set up 8 on the top and 5 on the bottom.)* Oh…we could pretend the 8 is 10, and then subtract 2!

Author's Notes

As Nina listens, she notes how children use known facts. Often the doubles are familiar.

Strategies are often "hidden" in children's work. Here the ten plus or minus strategy is used. Nina encourages Suzanne to examine when it is helpful and later challenges her to use it with eight.

Preparing for the Math Congress

After a sufficient amount of time has been spent on the game, ask children to consider which strategies they found helpful as they played, and explain that this will be the topic of discussion in the math congress. Ask the children to bring their arithmetic racks to the meeting area.

☀ Plan for a congress discussion that will highlight the strategies children found most helpful as they played the game.

▨ Tips for Structuring the Math Congress

The focus of the congress will be on strategies that children found helpful. A good way to structure this discussion is to start with a new problem and ask the children to use their arithmetic racks to solve it. Then have them share the strategies they found helpful.

Facilitating the Math Congress

☀ Present a new bus stop problem and ask the children to use their arithmetic racks to solve it.

☀ As children share their strategies, use the arithmetic rack to model their thinking.

Ask everyone to solve the following problem: "Four passengers are on the bus and eight people enter the bus at the next stop. How many passengers are on the bus as it leaves the bus stop?" Use the class-size rack to represent children's strategies.

Inside One Classroom

A Portion of the Math Congress

Theo: I put all 4 people on the top deck. They like it there because it's sunny. Then 8 people get on. There are 6 empty seats on the top deck, so 6 people go there and 2 go to the lower deck. This means that there are 10 and 2, and that's 12 people riding the bus.

Nina (the teacher): Let me use the big arithmetic rack to show what Theo just said, so everyone can see. You said 4 passengers went to the top deck. Here they are. *(Moves 4 beads.)* Next you said 6 people enter the bus and go to the top deck, and 2 people enter and go to the lower deck.

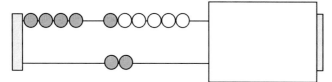

Here are the 8 people. So how do we know how many people are on the bus? How did Theo know?

Jolie: There are 10 passengers on the top deck—that's 5 red and 5 white. And 2 on the bottom. We just know 10 and 2 is 12. I did it sort of the same and sort of different. I had 4 people on the top, too. The 8 people got on and sat together on the bottom deck. *(She shows it on the large rack.)* Then I made 2 people come down. That made 2 on the top and 10 on the bottom.

Author's Notes

In their answers the children show how they use different strategies. Knowing six upper deck seats are still empty does not involve subtraction; it's obvious from the arithmetic rack. Splitting eight into six and two does involve subtraction or the use of known number facts.

By moving two passengers from the upper deck to the lower deck, Jolie uses a combination of compensation (4 + 8 = 2 + 10) and making ten as a strategy.

Reflections on the Day

Today, the children worked with addition using the arithmetic rack. Children will likely have used a variety of strategies: making ten, compensation, doubles, and near doubles. During math congress they discussed the advantages of several strategies. Like mathematicians, they are learning to look to the numbers before deciding on a strategy.

Subtraction on the Arithmetic Rack

Today the children will investigate subtraction situations using the arithmetic rack. They will play a new version of the Bus Stop game, this one focused on subtraction. And they will discuss different strategies that they can use to solve each bus stop situation.

Day Seven Outline

Developing the Context

* Present a bus scenario focused on subtraction, and have children discuss their thinking in pairs.

* As children share their strategies, use the arithmetic rack to model their thinking.

* Explain that children will play a new version of Bus Stop today.

Supporting the Investigation

* Note the subtraction strategies children use as they play the game.

Preparing for the Math Congress

* Plan for a congress discussion that will highlight the strategies children found most helpful as they played the game.

Facilitating the Math Congress

* Present a new bus stop problem and ask the children to use their arithmetic racks to solve it.

* As children share their strategies, use the arithmetic rack to model their thinking.

Materials Needed

The Double-Decker Bus (Appendix A)

Class-size arithmetic rack

Individual arithmetic rack—one per child

Bus Stop game cards (subtraction) (Appendix M)—one deck per group of two or three children

Blank Bus Stop game cards *(optional)* (Appendix K)

Developing the Context

- Present a bus scenario focused on subtraction, and have children discuss their thinking in pairs.

- As children share their strategies, use the arithmetic rack to model their thinking.

- Explain that children will play a new version of Bus Stop today.

Ask children to form partnerships with someone they are sitting next to. Pass out individual arithmetic racks, one per pair of children. Remind the children of the girl and her father in the story. Her father drives around and people get on and off the bus. Have them picture the following:

The girl's dad is driving around. He is approaching the next stop, and he knows there are thirteen passengers on the bus. At the stop, seven people leave and no one gets on. He wants to know how many passengers are still aboard.

Give the children time to solve the problem in pairs. Ask some to share their thinking. Use the class-size arithmetic rack to show what they did.

Explain that the class will play a new version of Bus Stop today, with people getting off the bus instead of on. Pass out materials and allow children to begin playing the game.

Developing the Context

Inside One Classroom

Author's Notes

Jolie: We have 10 on the top and 3 on the bottom. That is 13. But 7 people up top came down and got off. And now there are 3 and 3. And that is 6.

Nina: Let's see if we can follow you. You put 10 and 3 on the arithmetic rack. Like this?

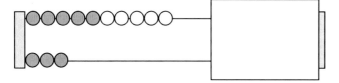

Nina uses the large rack to model the strategy for all to see. Jolie subtracts all seven passengers from the top deck.

And you removed 7 from the top bar. So you ended up with this?

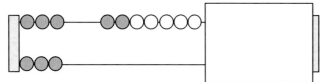

And here are your 6 passengers. *(Points at the 3 + 3 beads on the left.)*

Jolie: Yes, that's what we did. We know 3 and 3 makes 6. We just know that. But now I see another way, too.

Nina: Great, you have more than one way to solve it. Let's listen to other children. Did any of you solve this differently?

Mathematicians have a variety of strategies in their repertoire. They look to the numbers first to decide on an efficient strategy. Nina applauds Jolie for having more than one way but gives other children an opportunity to articulate their thinking.

continued on next page

continued from previous page

Max: We did the same—13 is 10 and 3. But the people on the bottom left the bus. And then 4 came down and got off the bus too.

Nina: Let's see, you did this?

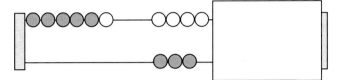

Max splits the seven passengers into four and three.

Another possible strategy is to split the thirteen passengers in such a way that you can easily remove seven of them.

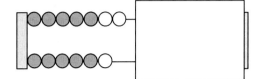

Max: Yeah. See, 3 and 4 is 7; those are the passengers who leave the bus. And 5 and 1 is 6—there are still 6 passengers on board.

Object of the Game

The purpose of the game is to encourage children to examine a variety of ways that the same number of passengers can be seated on the bus, and to explore the fact that some arrangements are easier than others to recognize and that these can be very helpful when subtracting.

Directions for Playing Bus Stop

The game is played in groups of two or three, and each player has an individual arithmetic rack. Cards are set up as they are in Bus Stop, the addition version (described on Day Six, page 40), with the deck of subtraction Bus Stop cards (Appendix M) stacked face down. Players take turns turning over a card from the stack. All players arrange the beads on their arithmetic racks to reflect the number of passengers on the bus (printed in the bus on the card) when it arrives at the bus stop. They then use the rack, either visually or by actually moving beads, to decide how many passengers remain on the bus as it pulls away. The children then compare how they placed the passengers on the bus and how they solved the subtraction story.

Behind the Numbers

As children play discourage them from simply removing the number of beads that are indicated and counting the remaining beads. An important goal of the game is to encourage children to think in small chunks, and to start visualizing this without actually removing the beads. To accomplish this ask them to imagine where the passengers are sitting and to think about how the colors of the seats and the two decks might be helpful.

Supporting the Investigation

As children play, move around and note the strategies they use for addition and subtraction. Note how they are arranging the beads on the racks. Confer with groups and support them as needed. (You can make additional cards, if needed, using the blank game cards in Appendix K.)

☀ Note the subtraction strategies children use as they play the game.

Listen in on the children's conversations and observe what strategies they use. Do they make use of the five- and ten-structures? Do they use addition and subtraction flexibly, understanding the connection between them? Do they use doubles or other known facts? Note the landmark strategies and big ideas they are developing for subtraction. Continue to map out the journey—the pathways—each child is making and note it on the landscape of learning graphic. Do you have evidence for everyone yet? This is a nice place in the unit to reflect about the children for whom you don't have much evidence of learning. As the unit progresses, make sure that you give them the attention necessary.

Preparing for the Math Congress

● Plan for a congress discussion that will highlight the strategies children found most helpful as they played the game.

After a sufficient amount of time has been spent on the game, ask children to think about the strategies they found helpful as they played, and explain that this will be the topic of discussion in the math congress.

Facilitating the Math Congress

● Present a new bus stop problem and ask the children to use their arithmetic racks to solve it.

● As children share their strategies, use the arithmetic rack to model their thinking.

Have children bring their arithmetic racks to the meeting area. Ask everyone to solve the following bus stop scenario: "There are 14 people on the bus and 8 people get off at the next stop. How many people are on the bus as it leaves the bus stop?" Ask children to share their solutions. Facilitate a conversation on the strategies as you did on Day Six. Children might use several strategies.

✦ There are 10 on top and 4 on the bottom. Eight people from the top deck leave the bus, so 2 on top and 4 on the bottom remain.

✦ There are 8 people on the top deck and 6 on the bottom. All 8 passengers from the top deck get off the bus.

✦ Seven on the top and 7 on the bottom. Seven from the bottom and 1 from the top leave, so 6 on the bottom remain.

In each case, you can discuss questions like, "Why did you put people on the bus that way?" "How do you know how many people remain on the bus?"

Reflections on the Day

Today children explored subtraction on the arithmetic rack. They are learning to relate addition to subtraction, to use facts they know to solve for subtraction, and to use the five- and ten-structures. During the math congress, they discussed the advantages of each strategy.

DAY EIGHT

Writing Bus Stories

Today and on Day Nine the children work in pairs writing addition and subtraction stories, using the context of people getting on and off a bus. The children will solve each other's math stories; cumulatively, the stories can be compiled into a math book. This project will help the children use the computation strategies they have learned so far, and will offer you opportunities for further assessment as you work toward completion of this unit.

Day Eight Outline

Developing the Context

☀ Use the story template to model for children how to create their own bus stories.

Supporting the Investigation

☀ Help children choose numbers for their stories that are appropriate for their working levels.

☀ Note children's strategies as they construct their stories.

Preparing for the Math Congress

☀ Plan for a congress discussion that will highlight the use of efficient strategies.

Facilitating the Math Congress

☀ Share and discuss some of the children's stories, highlighting a few different strategies children used.

Materials Needed

Class-size arithmetic rack

Individual arithmetic rack—one per pair of children

Instructions for making a story template (Appendix N)—one per pair of children

Markers

Developing the Context

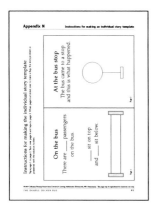

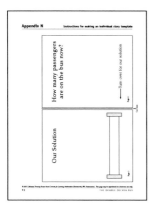

Use the class-size story template to model for children how to create their own bus stories.

Remind the children of the bus stories they have heard the last few days. Tell them that today the class will be writing a bus story together. "Let's imagine a double-decker bus. How might passengers on the bus be seated?" Take a few suggestions, and select one to record on a story template (Appendix N). Ask how that arrangement would be recorded on the blank arithmetic rack on the template. "The bus pulls up at a bus stop. What could happen at the bus stop?" Take a few suggestions—people getting on, people getting off, and people getting both on and off. Select one suggestion to record on the story template. Show how the right side of the story template will fold over to show the question, "How many passengers are on the bus now?"

Ask children to solve the math problem mentally and share strategies for figuring it out. Model the scenario using the arithmetic rack. Then record the new bus scenario, both in words and by drawing the bead arrangements on the story template as shown below:

On the bus	At the bus stop	Our solution	Question
There are 12 passengers on the bus: 5 sit on top and 7 sit below.	The bus came to a stop and this is what happened. 7 people got on the bus.	Now there are 19 passengers on the bus.	(Fold over and write question on back) *How many passengers are on the bus now?*
	+7		

Assign math partners, distribute the story template (Appendix N) to each pair of children, and ask them to invent a bus story together and solve it using their arithmetic racks. After they can comfortably tell their story, they will work together to write their stories on the story templates.

Supporting the Investigation

Help children choose numbers for their stories that are appropriate for their working levels.

Note children's strategies as they construct their stories.

Working with partners, children will decide what numbers to use and what happens at the bus stop. As you confer, advise them to use numbers that are challenging, and remind them that there is room for only twenty passengers on the bus. You might also want to post the spelling of words like *passenger, many,* and *bus driver* to make it easier for children to write the stories.

Depending on your children's ease and experiences with writing, you can encourage invented spelling or you might have them write a first draft or dictate their story, and then write the final draft yourself to make it easier for other children to read. Or you can change the template to include a basic story line with blanks for the numbers. In any case, the children should be able to tell the story and solve it themselves, with or without the support of the arithmetic rack.

When children finish one story, they can exchange stories with another pair and solve each other's problems, or they can write another bus story. Recommend that they choose another kind of problem for their next story—if they chose an addition situation for their first story, encourage them to consider subtraction or perhaps even a combination of addition and subtraction for their next story.

Assessment Tips

As children write, consider the growth and development of each child.

+ Do they write and solve addition or subtraction stories or stories in which people get both on and off the bus?

+ What numbers do the children use—small or large numbers, friendly or less friendly numbers? What does their choice of numbers say about their mathematical level?

+ What strategies do the children use to solve the bus stories? Are they counting by ones? Are they using groups of five? Are they using strategies like making ten or compensation? Do children think flexibly about a problem, using more than one way of solving it?

Differentiating Instruction

Different children will be challenged by different number problems. Some children will be challenged by addition situations with small numbers; allow these children to write stories such as "There are 7 passengers on board, and 5 more people get on." Others might prefer to use larger numbers (e.g., 18 passengers are on the bus and 13 get off). Some children will want to use combinations with passengers boarding and leaving the bus (e.g., 13 passengers on board, 9 leave and then 12 get on). When you assign partners, remember that while children learn from each other's strategies, it can be counterproductive if there is too big a gap between their working levels.

Preparing for the Math Congress

As you observe the children at work, think about which stories you will want to share with the class and why. Try to find stories that promote the making of groups of five and ten passengers. You might choose a child to share who started counting by ones but then discovered a more efficient way, or a child who used compensation ($9 + 8 = 10 + 7$).

☀ Plan for a congress discussion that will highlight the use of efficient strategies.

Facilitating the Math Congress

☀ Share and discuss some of the children's stories, highlighting a few different strategies children used.

Convene the children in the meeting area. Ask a pair to read their bus story aloud, but not the answer. Give the other children time to figure out how many passengers are on board as the bus leaves the stop. Share a few different strategies that children used.

After solving the problem, go back to the story page and ask whether the story is clearly written. Were there any parts that were confusing? Does the picture of the arithmetic rack match the story? How might the story be improved for the reader? Remind the children to keep these questions in mind as they continue to work on their own stories on Day Nine.

Reflections on the Day

Today the children started writing number stories about the double-decker bus, using addition, subtraction, or both. In choosing numbers for their own bus stories and in solving the problems posed in other children's stories, they had many opportunities to consider a variety of computation strategies. The context of the bus pushes children to use groups of five and ten, as well as strategies like compensation and doubles, when working with numbers less than twenty.

Writing Bus Stories

The children will warm up with quick images and then visualize adding and subtracting numbers on the arithmetic rack. Next, they continue working on bus stories and solving the problems contained in each other's stories, and they prepare to share their work with the class on Day Ten.

Day Nine Outline

Minilesson: Quick Images

☀ Show and discuss some quick image arrangements of beads on the arithmetic rack designed to encourage the use of doubles and/or groups of five or ten.

☀ Use the arithmetic rack to introduce some addition and subtraction problems.

Developing the Context

☀ Have children finish or revise their stories from Day Eight and then write one or more new stories.

Supporting the Investigation

☀ When all groups have written at least one story, have children read and solve the problems posed in each other's stories.

Preparing for the Math Congress

☀ Plan for a congress discussion that will highlight a range of addition and subtraction strategies.

Facilitating the Math Congress

☀ Note children's strategies as they solve each other's stories.

Materials Needed

Class-size arithmetic rack, with cover-up board

Individual arithmetic rack—one per pair of children

Children's bus stories from Day Eight

Instructions for making a story template (Appendix N)—two per pair of children

Minilesson: Quick Images (10–15 minutes)

● Show and discuss some quick image arrangements of beads on the arithmetic rack designed to encourage the use of doubles and/or groups of five or ten.

● Use the arithmetic rack to introduce some addition and subtraction problems.

Start with quick images on the class-size arithmetic rack; then move on to visually adding or removing quantities. Choose a few quick images from the list below. Prepare the number on the class-size arithmetic rack, show the image for a few seconds, and then cover it up. Have children briefly share one or two strategies for figuring out the total number of beads shown in each image, making sure that the idea of fives is brought up.

Behind the Numbers

Two possible strategies are using groups of five, or using doubles. For instance, 7 + 8 can be seen as 5 red and 5 red and 5 white or as 7 and 7 and 1 more. Showing the numbers as a quick image discourages counting each bead. The children have to break the number into parts to reconstruct a visualization of the amount. Using groups of five and ten, using doubles, or counting back from 20 are common strategies.

3 on the top, 5 on the bottom

4 on the top, 5 on the bottom

7 on the top, 5 on the bottom

7 on the top, 8 on the bottom

9 on the top, 7 on the bottom

9 on the top, 6 on the bottom

9 on the top, 5 on the bottom

Now introduce some addition and subtraction problems. Starting off with a quick image, tell the children what the change is, and ask how they figured it out. For example, try these combinations:

Briefly show 3 on top, 5 on the bottom. Say:
"Five passengers enter the bus. How many now?"

Briefly show 7 on top, 9 on the bottom. Say:
"Five passengers leave the bus. How many now?"

Briefly show 8 on top, 9 on the bottom. Say:
"Ten passengers leave the bus. How many now?"

Developing the Context

● Have children finish or revise their stories from Day Eight and then write one or more new stories.

Remind the children of the bus stories they wrote on Day Eight. Explain that they will continue working with them today in order to have a large number of stories for a class book. Have the children work in the same pairs as on Day Eight. Give them time to finish or revise their first stories and to write one or more new stories.

Supporting the Investigation

● When all groups have written at least one story, have children read and solve the problems posed in each other's stories.

Guidance for today's work might be mathematical ("Try solving stories in more than one way. You and your partner should agree on the answer before recording it") or editorial ("Look over your work and make sure it makes sense"). Remind the children of any helpful tips that came up at the close of the workshop on Day Eight.

Children who finish quickly can challenge themselves by writing more stories. When all groups have written at least one story, have the children read and solve the problems posed in the other children's stories.

As the end of work time nears, let the children know they should put finishing touches on their completed bus stories. Tell them there will be a "gallery walk" of everyone's work on Day Ten. In the gallery walk, children will display their stories and have an opportunity to read each other's stories.

▨ Assessment Tips

As children work on their stories, consider their growth and development.

+ Do they write and solve addition or subtraction stories or stories in which people get both on and off the bus?

+ What numbers do the children use—small or large numbers, friendly or less friendly numbers? What does their choice of numbers tell you about their mathematical thinking?

+ What strategies do the children use to solve the bus stories? Are they counting by ones? Are they using groups of five? Are they using strategies like making ten or compensation? Do children think flexibly about problems, using more than one way of solving them?

+ Do they relate addition and subtraction?

Preparing for the Math Congress

Listen in as children read bus stories and solve the problems they pose. Look for stories that allow different strategies, for problems that trigger discussions among the children. Such problems help children rethink and reflect on their strategies. Also look for problems that children find easy to solve. These latter problems will allow children to celebrate their own growth and development.

☀: Plan for a congress discussion that will highlight a range of addition and subtraction strategies.

Facilitating the Math Congress

Convene the children in the meeting area, bringing their arithmetic racks and one bus story. Invite pairs of children to share their stories. Allow the other children time to solve the bus problem, using the arithmetic rack as a model for thinking if they choose. Watch how children are moving the beads. Do they move them by one at a time or in clusters? Do they count them or do they just know at a glance how many there are?

☀: Note children's strategies as they solve each other's stories.

A Portion of the Math Congress

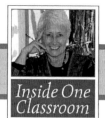

Author's Notes

Mei and Theo have collaborated on this bus story.

Mei: It rained all day, and the bus is almost full. There were 9 people on the top deck and they had gotten wet. The 7 people downstairs were happy.

Theo: It was crowded at the bus stop—12 people were waiting. Then 11 people left the bus and the 12 people got on. How many people are on the bus now?

Nina (the teacher): A lot happens in this story. Let's take time to solve it first. *(Wait time.)* All right, who would like to share your thinking?

Nina provides time for thinking and notices how the children are solving the problem.

Max: This is hard. There were 9 on top and 7 below—that's like 10 on top and 6 on the bottom, which is 16. So 12 people can't get on because there isn't enough room. But then 11 people leave the bus— maybe all 9 from the top because they are wet and don't like it, and 2 from the bottom. So there are 5 people left on the bus. Now 12 people can get on—10 on the top and 2 on the bottom. That's 17.

Max uses compensation to figure the initial number of passengers, imagining one passenger moving upstairs ($9 + 7 = 10 + 6$). When twelve passengers get on, he considers that $5 + 12 = 10 + 2 + 5 = 10 + 7$.

Sophia: I did it a different way. First there were 16 people. If 12 get on and 11 leave, that's just like one more person getting on. And $16 + 1$ is 17.

Sophia has mathematized the problem. She is thinking beyond the context of passengers getting on and off the bus and is manipulating numbers. She uses the associative property: $(16 - 11) + 12 = 16 + (-11 + 12)$.

Reflections on the Day

Today's work began with quick images to reinforce groupings of five and ten. As addition and subtraction situations were introduced within the context of the double-decker bus, children were encouraged to use grouping strategies that were suggested by the earlier quick images. Children then continued writing and sharing bus stories. One or two stories were shared in the congress, highlighting different addition and subtraction strategies.

Sharing Bus Stories

Today children enjoy a gallery walk. They spend half the time reading and solving the problems in other children's stories and half the time answering questions and explaining their own solution strategies to their classmates.

Day Ten Outline

Supporting the Investigation

☀ Listen and watch for evidence of growth and development as children discuss their own bus stories and solve the math problems contained in each other's stories.

Preparing for the Math Congress

☀ Plan for a congress that will highlight an interesting variety of strategies.

Facilitating the Math Congress

☀ Use the math congress as an opportunity for you and the children to reflect on and celebrate their mathematical development.

Minilesson: A String of Related Problems

☀ Work on a string of related addition problems that encourage children to use the five- and ten-structures.

☀ Use the arithmetic rack to model children's thinking.

Materials Needed

Children's bus stories from Days Eight and Nine

Before class, display all the stories around the meeting area.

Class-size arithmetic rack

Individual arithmetic rack—one per child

Large chart pad and easel

Markers

Supporting the Investigation

☀ Listen and watch for evidence of growth and development as children discuss their own bus stories and solve the math problems contained in each other's stories.

Children prepare to share their bus stories and explain how they solved their problems. The share is set up as a gallery walk with all the work displayed simultaneously. The stories can be posted on the wall or displayed on tables. Each partnership decides who will host visitors first and who will visit and solve other children's stories first. Halfway through the gallery walk, the children in each pair switch positions: the hosts become visitors, and visitors become hosts.

As visitors, children walk around with their arithmetic racks, reading and solving everyone else's bus stories. Each child explains to the host/author how he or she solved their problem, and then listens to the host/author's own strategy for reaching a solution. Hosts will decipher any words or clarify anything that may be unclear, and they explain to visitors their own strategy for solving the problem. They also have the opportunity to hear others solve the same problem.

▣ Assessment Tips

As children discuss their own bus stories and solve the math problems contained in each other's stories, listen and watch for evidence of growth and development:

✦ What strategies are children using to solve addition problems? Subtraction problems? Problems involving both addition and subtraction?

✦ How have their strategies changed over the course of the week? Is there evidence of growth?

✦ Are children using the arithmetic rack and, if so, how? Do they use the rack in a deliberate way, moving and counting the beads? Do they look at the rack and visualize numbers, without actually moving the beads?

✦ Are the children solving the problems mentally? Are they using structures of five and ten in their computation?

✦ Is there evidence that children are mathematizing—that they are thinking of and acting on numbers removed from the context?

Preparing for the Math Congress

☀ Plan for a congress that will highlight an interesting variety of strategies.

In preparation for the last congress of the unit, look for evidence of children's growth. During the gallery walk, collect anecdotes that you can share with the group, or ask children to share moments of enlightenment. Look for a story that drew an interesting variety of strategies or discussion.

Facilitating the Math Congress

This is an opportunity for you and the children to reflect on and celebrate their mathematical development. For instance, "Wendy solved our bus story in a totally different way than we did. At first I didn't get it and she had to tell me two more times. But then I realized what she meant and I thought it was a good way to think about our story." Or you can share observations about the whole group: "When we started working with bus stories a few days ago, many of you were using your rack to solve all the problems. Now you're solving stories in two or three ways, sometimes entirely in your head. What a big difference."

☀ Use the math congress as an opportunity for you and the children to reflect on and celebrate their mathematical development.

Minilesson: A String of Related Problems (10–15 minutes)

Close the math congress with a minilesson involving just numbers, without a story context. You will not be displaying the problems on the arithmetic rack, only writing them. The rack is used only as a model as children share their strategies. You might say, "We've been spending a lot of time thinking about passengers on these buses and ways of adding and subtracting them. Now let's think about how that can help us solve math problems that are just numbers."

The minilesson is crafted with a string of related addition problems that encourage children to use the five-structure. Write one problem at a time on chart paper. Children are free to use their individual arithmetic racks or to look at the class-size arithmetic rack. Give the children think time—ask them to show when they have finished thinking by giving a thumbs-up signal. Ask one child to share his or her thinking, using the class-size arithmetic rack to model the strategy. Explore various strategies. Children will usually make connections between the problems in this addition string. If they don't, ask explicitly how these problems are related. You will certainly want to highlight any use of the five-structure or strategies such as doubles and compensation.

☀ Work on a string of related addition problems that encourage children to use the five- and ten-structures.

☀ Use the arithmetic rack to model children's thinking.

String of related problems:

5 + 5

5 + 6

7 + 3

7 + 8

8 + 5

8 + 6

9 + 7

Behind the Numbers

The first problem reminds children of the structure of the rack, even though the amounts are not displayed on the rack as an image. The answer to the second problem is just one more than the answer to the first, encouraging children to use what they know. The third and fourth problems are also related—the third sets the stage for the ten-structure, and the fourth encourages children to use it. The last three problems require children to make their own visualizations of the five- and ten-structures.

Reflections on the Unit

In *Through the Looking Glass*, the White Queen asks Alice, "Can you do addition? What's one and one and one and one and one and one and one and one and one and one?" Alice responds, "I don't know. I lost count." Like the White Queen, children begin thinking about addition by relying on counting individual units. To go beyond this initial counting strategy they must construct various big ideas and alternative strategies. When adding greater amounts, counting is insufficient. For example, to add all of the White Queen's ones with a strategy other than counting, one must group them into four and four and two, or 2 fives, etc. Strategies such as these are based on number sense.

Once children understand the big ideas involved in the operations of addition and subtraction, and can model various situations, it is important that they automatize the basic facts. In contrast to memorization, automaticity is accomplished by developing relationships among the facts, leaving far fewer facts to memorize. Repetitive drill and practice and the use of flashcards will not develop an understanding of relationships.

Facts that do need to be memorized are doubles and combinations that make ten, because they are the basis for critical landmark strategies such as using near doubles, making tens, using compensation, and using other known facts.

Manipulatives like connecting cubes or other counting materials do not necessarily support the development of these strategies. The arithmetic rack was specifically designed to support the development of children's addition and subtraction strategies. It can be used in minilessons or with contexts and routines. As children work with it, they are able to use strategies like near doubles, making tens, and compensation—they develop a better sense of the relationships among numbers. And it is the automaticity of facts and the development of number relationships that form the basis for efficient calculating and the further development of number theory.

This unit provided children with ample opportunities to develop a strong sense of number. They were encouraged to compose and decompose numbers, particularly making use of the five- and ten-structures. They explored addition and subtraction and discussed how they were related. As they worked with the arithmetic rack, they were supported in developing several strategies for automatizing the basic facts, such as using doubles, compensation, and making tens.

The minute I wake up, even before I open my eyes, I know it's a nice day out. I know because I can feel sun on my face and I can hear kids laughing and dogs barking and cars honking. I hop out of bed and settle in my window seat. Out my bedroom window all the world's a stage, and I have a front-row seat.

There's Mr. Peshkov, my downstairs neighbor, reading the paper on a bench. Mrs. Rivera is shopping with her baby at the fruit and vegetable stand. Matthew, who's walking his big dog, Brandy, sees me and waves.

The street is alive too. There are cars and delivery trucks, taxis and a couple of bicycles. And look, there it is—the double-decker bus!

I love double-decker buses. I love the red and white seats. I love the way you can sit on the top deck or the bottom deck. I like to sit on top, of course. There's no roof up there so the breeze blows in your face, and you can see the sky and the tops of the buildings and the trees. But most of all I love the double-decker buses because my daddy drives one.

When a double-decker bus comes by, I like to figure out how many passengers are on it. On this bus, I can see five people on the upper deck and four passengers on the lower deck. Sometimes the bus pulls away from the bus stop too soon and I don't have time to count them all. Still, I can figure it out because I know five plus five is ten. Five plus four is one less, so there are nine passengers on that bus.

I remember one day when the sky was really blue. It was so beautiful that even the birds were singing extra loudly. That day the top seats—all ten of them—were always full. Just a few people sat on the bottom deck. Maybe they wanted to sit on the upper deck, too, but there was no room—except for the lady with the gigantic straw hat and sunglasses. She probably just wanted to stay out of the sun.

I like it when Daddy tells me about the buses. "Sometimes," he says, "when people get on the bus, they ask if there are any seats on the upper deck. But I can't tell them because I can't see up there." I helped him figure it out. I told him if he knew how many people were on the bus altogether, he could just subtract the people he could see on the bottom. Then he would know how many were on the top. He liked my idea and he tried it. That night when Daddy came home from work, he told me the idea had worked!

"This morning," he explained, "I knew that eight passengers had boarded the bus. And I saw just two of them sitting behind me downstairs. So I figured that there must be six sitting upstairs. I know there are ten seats upstairs, so I was able to tell a lady who asked that there were four empty seats on top."

I felt proud that I could help my daddy.

On another day when Daddy came home, he told me that in the afternoon ten passengers were riding his bus, and all of them sat upstairs. "But then the sky got a little dark," he said, "and a few raindrops started falling. First a lady in a yellow sundress came down to the lower deck. I think she was cold. Then a man with a newspaper came down. His newspaper was already a little wet."

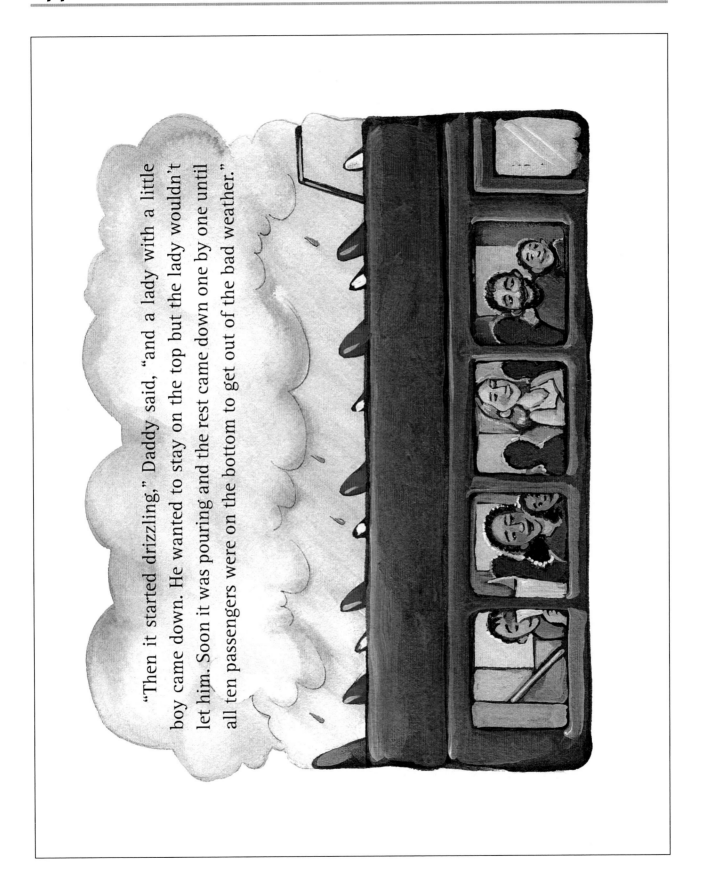

"Then it started drizzling," Daddy said, "and a lady with a little boy came down. He wanted to stay on the top but the lady wouldn't let him. Soon it was pouring and the rest came down one by one until all ten passengers were on the bottom to get out of the bad weather."

But today it's not raining. The sun is shining brightly on my face as I sit on my seat looking out the window. I think today everyone will rush to get the seats on the upper deck.

When I grow up I want to drive a bus, too, and greet the passengers and help them get where they're going. And when I do, it's definitely going to be a double-decker bus because that's twice as much fun.

To make a class-size arithmetic rack, find a large piece of cardboard, about three feet by one and a half feet. Punch four holes, two on each side, through the cardboard, approximately six inches apart top to bottom, but two feet across. Using wire or thin rope (such as clothesline), string twenty beads in two rows of ten (five of each color) as in the illustration below. Thread the wire or rope through the holes and twist or tie in the back. [Note: If you use wire, it is possible to use connecting cubes in place of beads.]

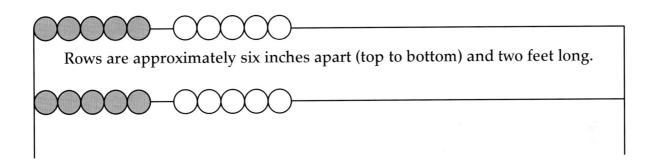

Rows are approximately six inches apart (top to bottom) and two feet long.

Individual arithmetic racks can be made in a similar fashion to the class-size arithmetic rack. Just use a smaller piece of cardboard, about four inches by twelve inches. Use shoelaces in place of wire and make sure that the beads you use are small enough to move easily along the shoelaces.

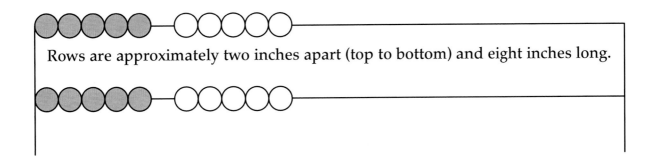

Rows are approximately two inches apart (top to bottom) and eight inches long.

Visit www.contextsforlearning.com for information on where to purchase arithmetic racks.

Appendix C — Student recording sheet for bus passenger arrangements

Names ____ Date ________________

__________ people on our bus

What we saw: ____

____

____

__________ people on our bus

What we saw ____

____

____

__________ people on our bus

What we saw ____

____

____

Names _____ Date _____

_____ people on our bus

The easy one   The hard one

_____ people on the top deck   _____ people on the top deck

_____ people on the bottom deck   _____ people on the bottom deck

_____ people on our bus

The easy one   The hard one

_____ people on the top deck   _____ people on the top deck

_____ people on the bottom deck   _____ people on the bottom deck

■ These cards can be made more durable by pasting them on oaktag and laminating them.

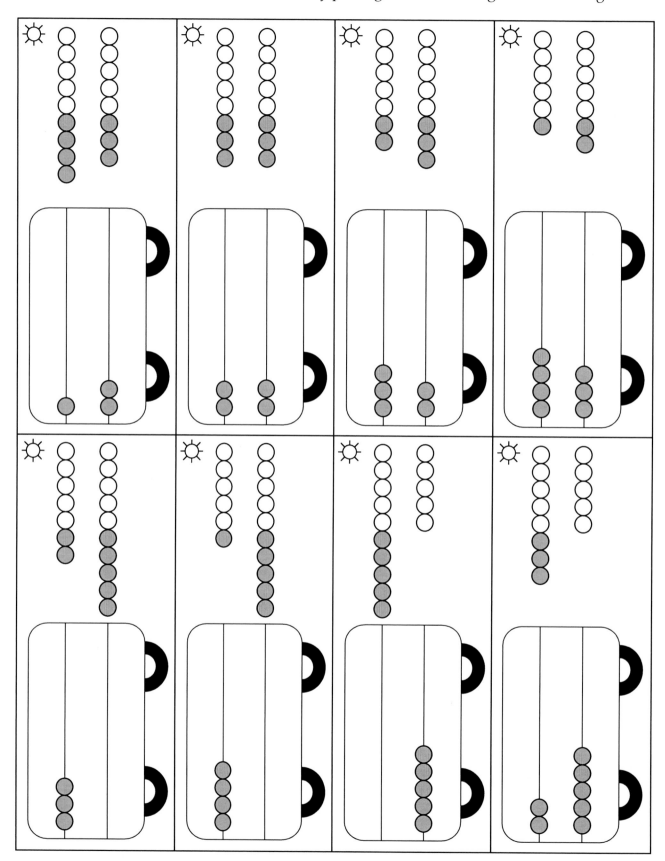

Appendix E

■ These cards can be made more durable by pasting them on oaktag and laminating them.

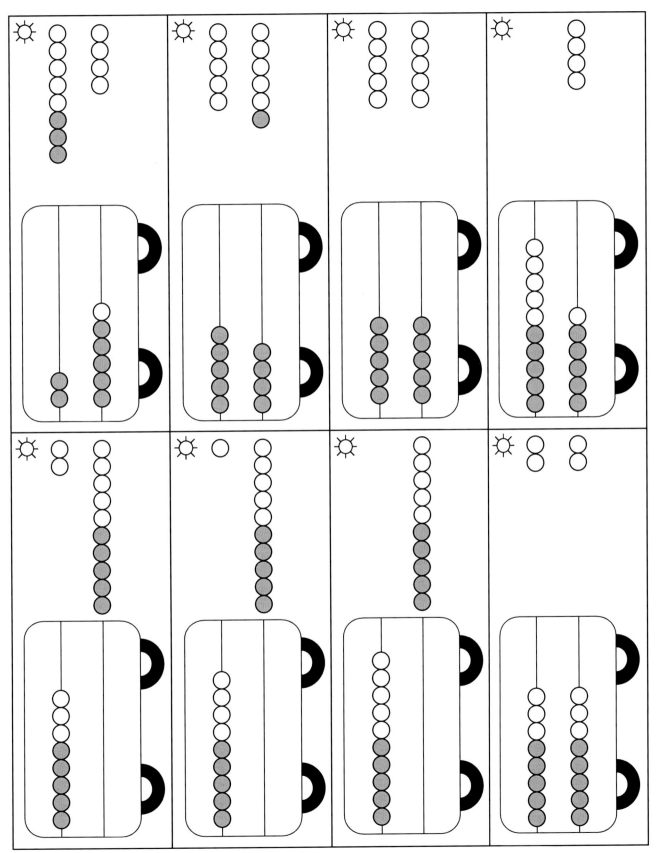

THE DOUBLE-DECKER BUS

Appendix E

■ These cards can be made more durable by pasting them on oaktag and laminating them.

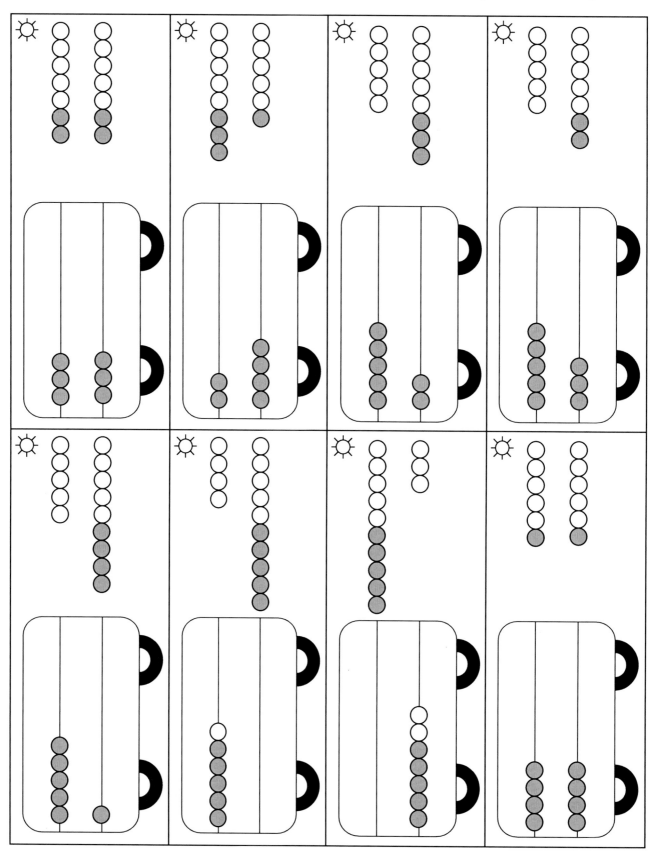

■ These cards can be made more durable by pasting them on oaktag and laminating them.

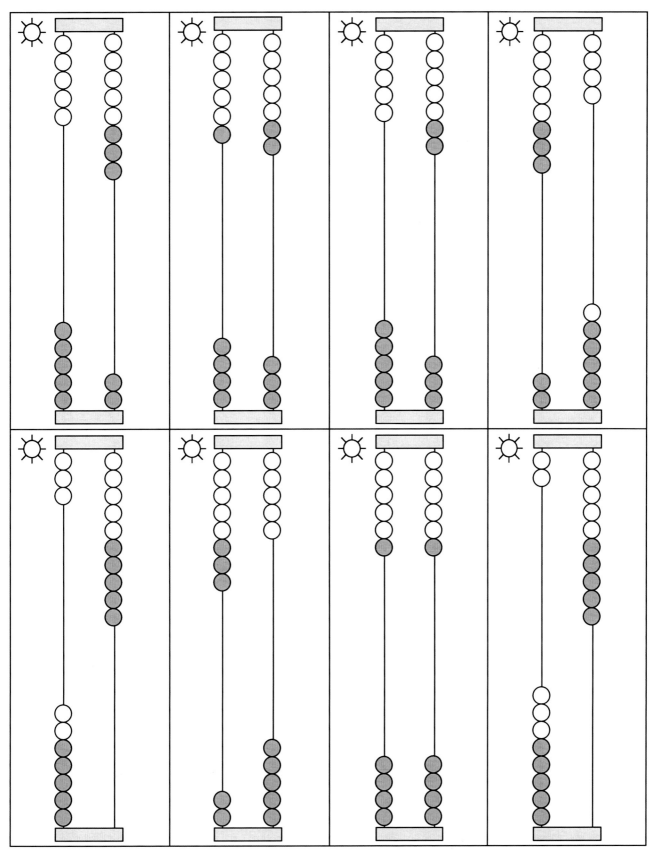

■ These cards can be made more durable by pasting them on oaktag and laminating them.

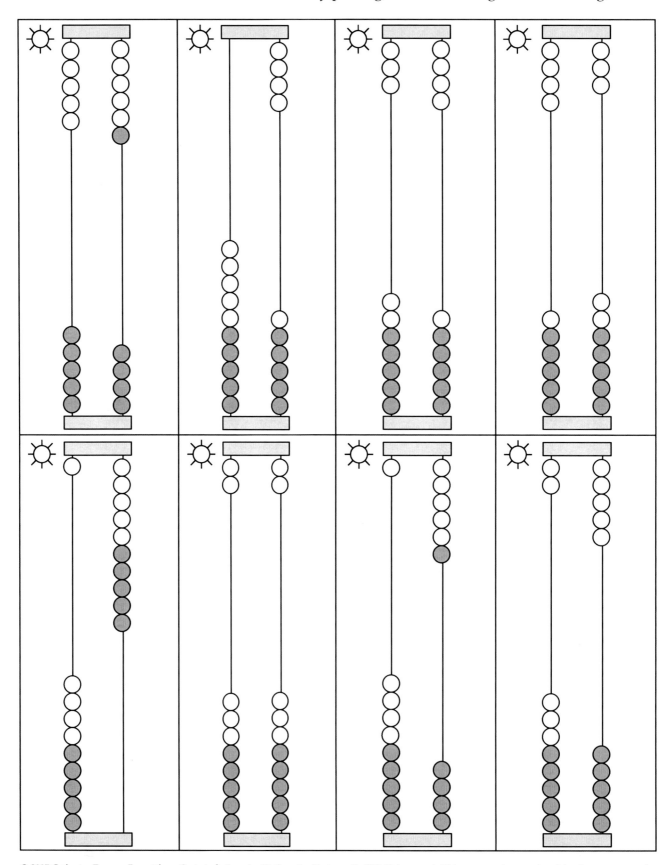

Appendix F

■ These cards can be made more durable by pasting them on oaktag and laminating them.

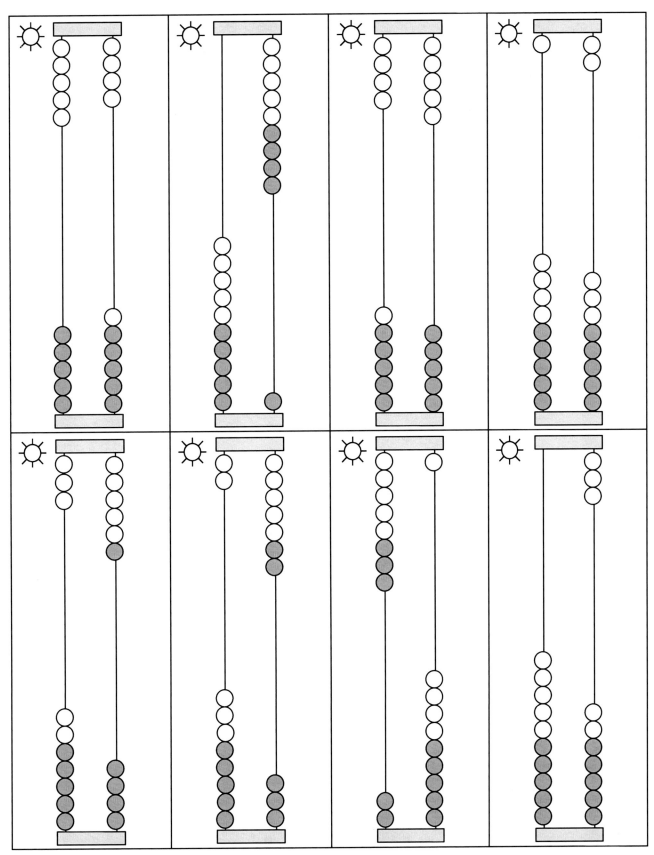

Here are some suggestions for quick image minilessons with the arithmetic rack:

Total number of beads	Beads on top	Beads on bottom
19	10	9
18	8	10
18	9	9
17	10	7
17	8	9
16	6	10
16	9	7
16	8	8
15	10	5
15	9	6
15	7	8
14	10	4
14	7	7
13	3	10
13	6	7
13	8	5
12	10	2
12	6	6
12	7	5
11	10	1
11	5	6
11	9	2
10	10	0
10	5	5
9	5	4
8	8	0
8	4	4
7	5	2
7	0	7
6	3	3

Appendix H

■ These cards can be made more durable by pasting them on oaktag and laminating them.

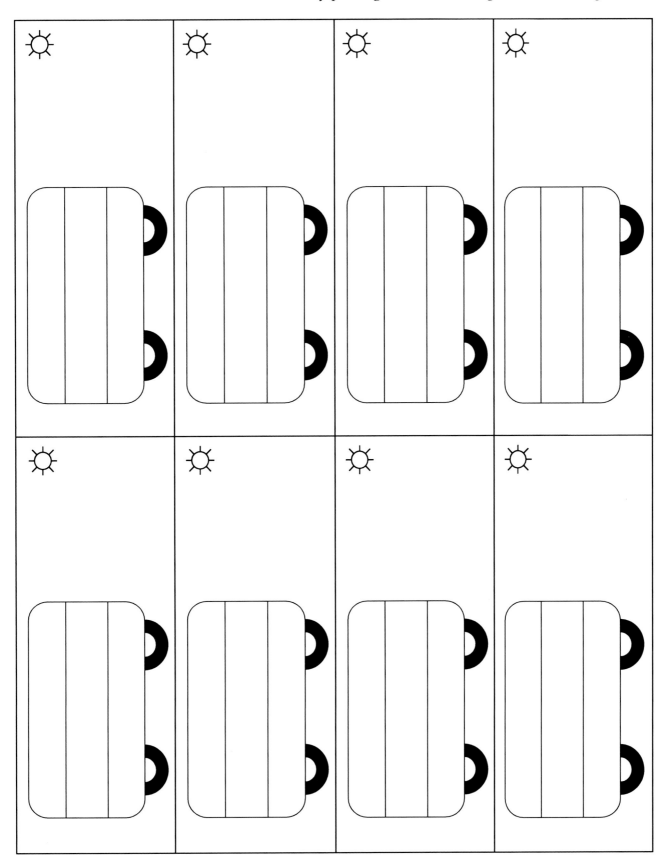

■ These cards can be made more durable by pasting them on oaktag and laminating them.

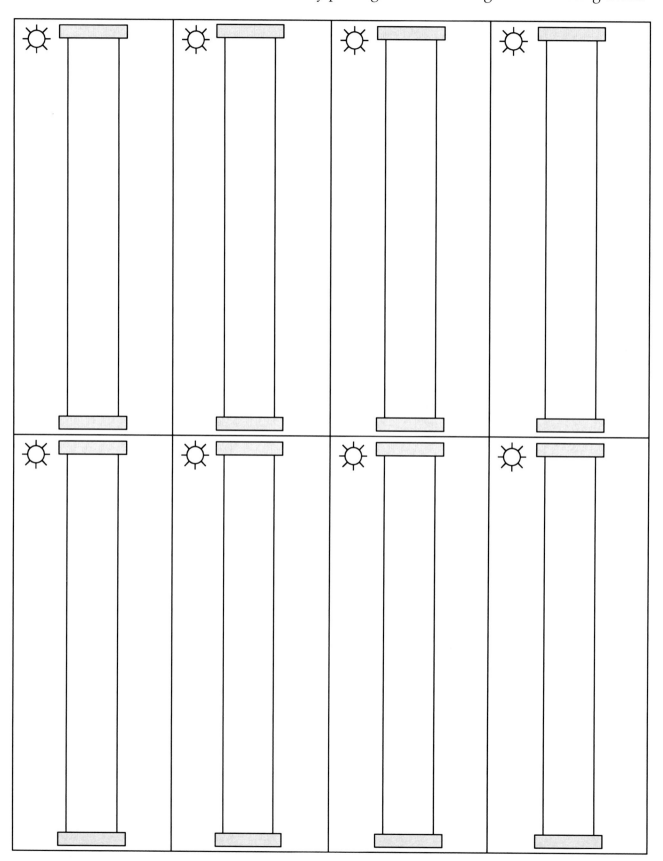

Name _____ Date _____

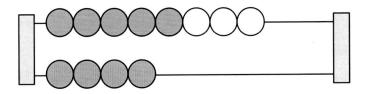 Empty seats on top_____

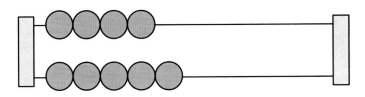 Empty seats on top_____

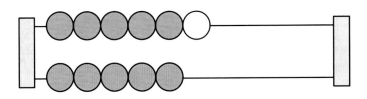 Empty seats on top_____

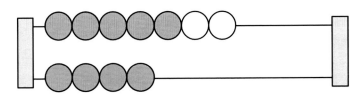 Empty seats on top_____

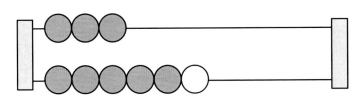 Empty seats on top_____

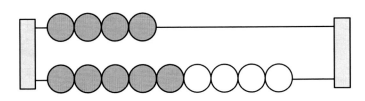 Empty seats on top_____

■ These cards can be made more durable by pasting them on oaktag and laminating them.

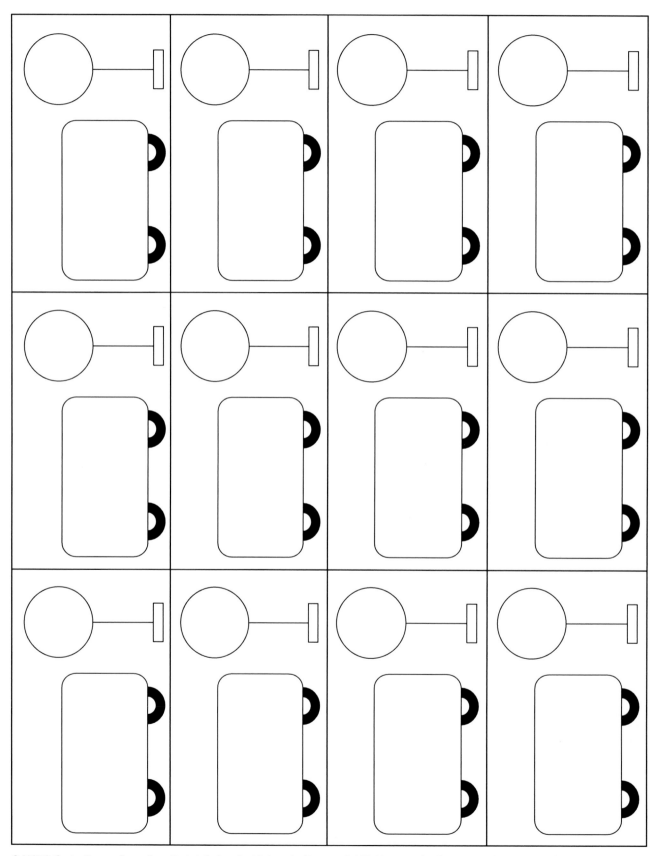

■ These cards can be made more durable by pasting them on oaktag and laminating them.

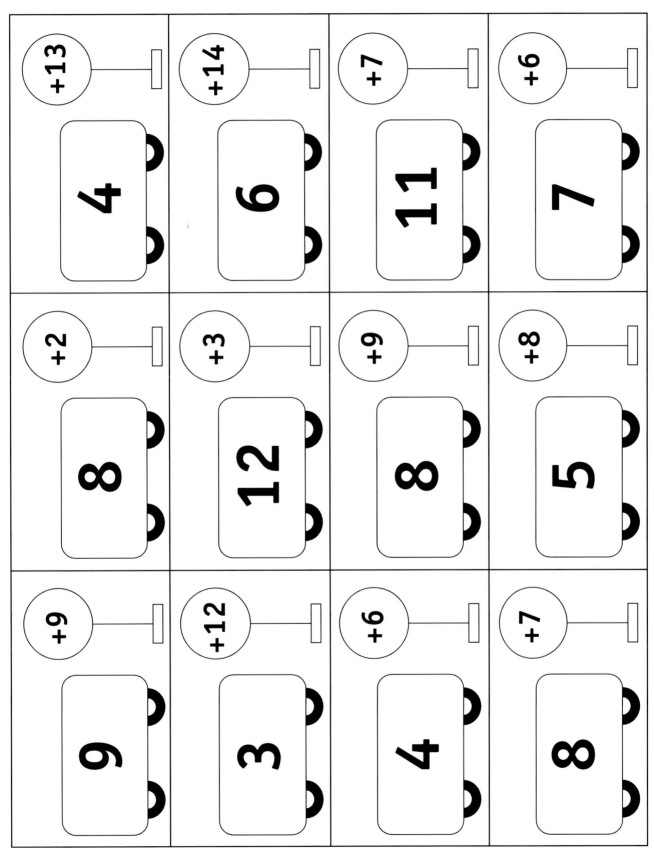

■ These cards can be made more durable by pasting them on oaktag and laminating them.

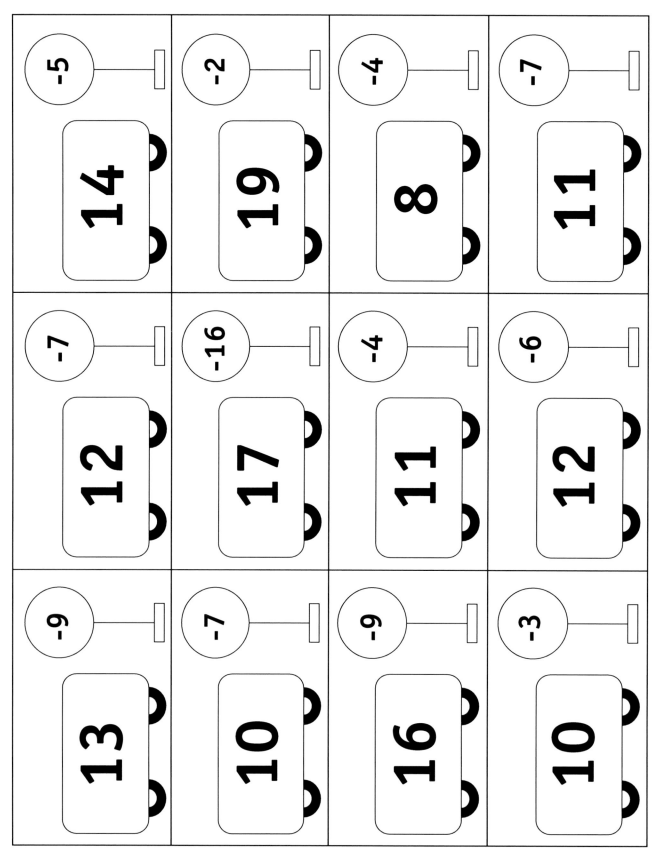

Instructions for making a story template

Tape page 3 to page 2. Turn over page 4 and tape to page 3. When page 4 is folded over to make a flap, the story problem is presented with the solution hidden.

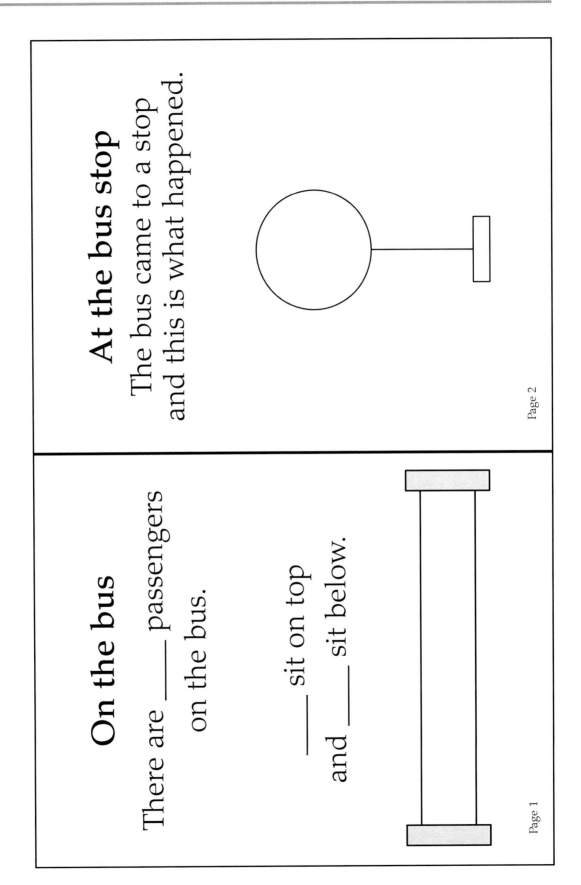

At the bus stop

The bus came to a stop
and this is what happened.

Page 2

On the bus

There are ____ passengers
on the bus.

____ sit on top
and ____ sit below.

Page 1

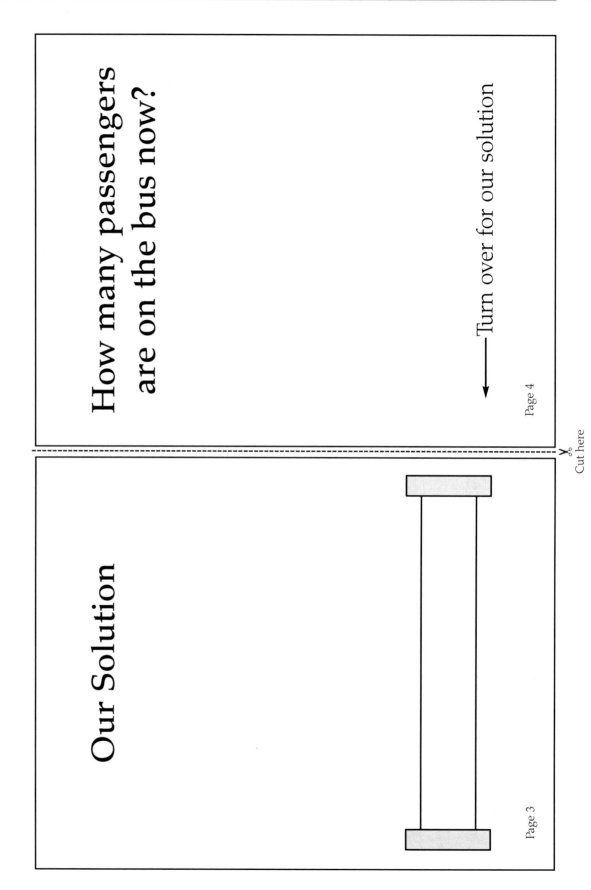

How many passengers are on the bus now?

Turn over for our solution

Page 4

Cut here

Our Solution

Page 3